LAST STANDS

FAMOUS BATTLES AGAINST THE ODDS

CRAIG PHILIP

DORSET PRESS

This edition published by
Dorset Press,
a division of Marboro Books Corp.,
by arrangement with Brompton Books Corporation

Produced by Brompton Books Corporation
15 Sherwood Place
Greenwich, CT 06830

ISBN 1-56619-467-9

Printed in China

CONTENTS

Introduction

"To those who flee comes neither power nor glory."

HOMER, THE ILIAD

THROUGHOUT THE HISTORY of warfare, the last stand against overwhelming odds has interested the soldier, historian, student, and general reader alike. Hundreds of books, plays, films and songs celebrate battles and sieges where outnumbered soldiers have stood fast against a vastly more powerful enemy.

Most attention has been paid to actions where small groups of men made the cold-blooded decision to fight and die, even when escape or surrender was possible, for such decisions have a resonance and fascination which echoes through the ages. But the definition of a "last stand" could be said to cover a much wider set of circumstances.

Sometimes the outnumbered force has decided that fighting gives them the best chance of survival. It could be that they have the advantage of a defendable position if they stay and fight, while they would be wiped out in the open if they tried to run. Other heroic stands have been made solely because of mis-

takes by politicians or generals, leaving the fighting men to try and make the best of an impossible situation. Perhaps the most common kind of last stand is where a group of people are under attack but have nowhere else to go. This is often the case when a city is under siege, where the defenders are fighting for their families, their homes, often their religion and sometimes their whole way of life. Here the last stand is not purely a military phenomenon, and large numbers of civilians and non-combatants also become involved.

The bonds that tie men (and sometimes women) together in such a desperate situation are varied. Studies of fighting soldiers show that it is the individual's loyalty to his immediate group that is the strongest incentive to keep fighting. A soldier will die for his comrades, for his platoon, or sometimes for his regiment, but rarely for his general or for his country. There have been cases where a heroic leader has inspired his men to great feats, but these tend to be where a smaller group is involved and the leader is personally known to the soldiers.

Culture and religion, of course, can also be important factors in inspiring heroism; and the threat of an enemy who is sworn to destroy a way of life, or suppress deeply held beliefs, can be a powerful incentive to keep fighting. Some societies even demand great sacrifices as part of their cultural tradition, often at the behest of a religious or tribal leader. The Japanese Army that fought in World War II is the best example of this idea. Consisting of men brought up to believe in self-sacrifice for the greater good, they were told, and indeed they believed, that losing the war would mean the destruction of their country, their God-Emperor and their way of life.

Occasionally, the result of a last stand has determined the outcome of a war, has heralded the end of a city, or as in Constantinople in 1453, the end of a civilization. Others have had little direct military effect, but instead have made a lasting impression on the minds of others. Some gallant sacrifices have inspired armies to victory, while others have left such scars that people have lost their will to fight. Whether a deliberate decision to die or a bitter struggle to survive, the heroism of the last stand has struck a chord with many through the ages, and will no doubt continue to do so as long as human beings are prepared to fight for their comrades, their families, their society or their freedom.

LEFT: The last stand of General George Custer was a direct result of this flamboyant publicity seeker's lack of caution.

FAR LEFT: During the seige of the Legations in Peking, a multi-national force fought their way through to save the diplomats. These Chinese were among those who tried to stop them.

Thermopylae

480 BC

"Have a good breakfast, men, for we dine in Hades."

KING LEONIDAS OF SPARTA

THE PERSIAN EMPIRE in 480 BC was a mighty conglomeration of peoples and nations, all responding to the will of one man, Xerxes, the King of Kings. Even so, there were continual problems with minor rebellions and with enemies on the outskirts of the empire, especially from those troublesome neighbors to the west, the Greeks. Xerxes had finally decided to crush these quarrelsome people once and for all, so in the spring of that year he launched an invasion of the Greek peninsula. An immense host of over 200,000 infantrymen, archers and cavalrymen, supported by a huge supply train and a fleet of over 600 ships, was to cross the Hellespont then pass through Thrace and Macedonia and down into the Greek mainland states and the Peloponnese.

RIGHT: This statue is supposedly of Leonidas, one of the Spartan kings. It shows him with the "Corinthian" style of crested helmet worn by Spartan officers.

BELOW: The standing figure on the left is Xerxes; his father Darius is seated.

A patchwork of tiny independent states made up the area now known as Greece, and most had a long history of fighting and arguing with their neighbors. Even as the Persians advanced, the grossly outnumbered Greeks argued over whether resistance was feasible, and if so, who would supply the troops, and where they should fight. Eventually, plans were made to abandon some of the southern cities, with whatever men available being sent north to block, or at the very least delay, the advancing armies.

This army would be led by Leonidas, one of the two kings of Sparta. His people were the Spartiates, a unique ruling elite that lived by a strict moral and religious code which emphasized duty above all else. Constantly training for war, they lived frugally in military-style messes, becoming imbued with a grim sense of honor and sacrifice. This tiny group had an uneasy and sometimes hostile relationship with their subject peoples, the *helots*, although many of these subjects would fight just as heroically as their masters in defense of their lands. Sparta's limited manpower resources and preoccupation with the religious festival of Carneia meant that Leonidas would be accompanied by a relatively small force, comprising 300 ranking Spartiates of the royal bodyguard and about 1000 *helots*. However, by the time the 1300 Spartans had marched to the chosen battleground at Thermopylae, they had been joined by some 7000 men from other Greek states, including contingents from Phocis, Thespiae, Thebes and Arcadia.

Thermopylae is on the east coast of northern Greece, a place where steep mountains reach down to the sea. In 480 BC, a single coastal track provided the only route south for a large army, winding past the sheer rocky slopes of Mount Killidromos. Three narrow passes, or "gates," restricted this track, the middle one only being some 20 to 30 yards wide – an ideal position for a small group of men to hold back a much larger army. By early August, the advance elements of Xerxes' army had reached this pass, with the main force just a few days behind. To their front, they could see the sun glinting off the polished bronze helmets and shields of the heavily armed Greek infantry (known as "hoplites") standing in formation behind a low ruined wall.

On the 18 August, the initial assault was launched. The troops chosen were the Medes, who fired arrows from close range then charged the grim, menacing rows of shielded, helmeted warriors. The Greeks were formed up in phalanxes, usually eight men deep, each phalanx probably being formed by men from a single city-state and officered by the Spartan elite. The men in the rear ranks would move forward to replace those in the front as they fell, or would change places between attacks to provide a fresh front line to face the next charge. Their shields and armor were largely impenetrable to the arrows and short spears of the Medes, while they were able to slice through the thin Persian mail armor with their bronze-tipped spears. This first assault eventually petered out, and the Medes withdrew, leaving piles of their dead and wounded lying in front of the Greek line. Next was the turn of the men from Susa, but this assault also spent its force against the rock-steady phalanxes.

RIGHT: Even after his hard-fought victory at Thermopylae and subsequent capture of Athens, Xerxes never succeeded in subduing the Greek people

The Persians were determined to clear the pass that day, so the elite royal guards, the "Immortals," were finally unleashed. The cream of Xerxes' army, these were the superbly trained shock troops that had proven their worth time and time again in the wars of the Persian empire. In this case, they also could only make

BELOW: A sixth century BC view of a Greek warrior. The men at Thermopylae had similar equipment, but with larger and completely circular shields.

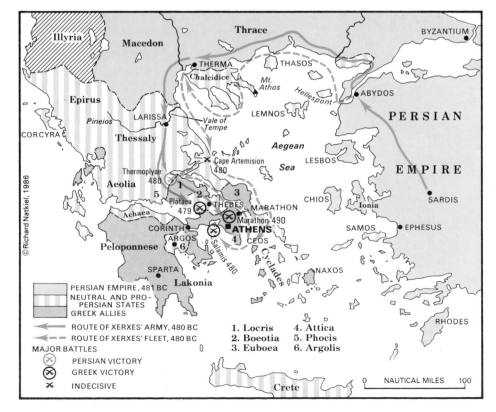

PERSIAN EMPIRE, 481 BC
NEUTRAL AND PRO-PERSIAN STATES
GREEK ALLIES

ROUTE OF XERXES' ARMY, 480 BC
ROUTE OF XERXES' FLEET, 480 BC
MAJOR BATTLES

PERSIAN VICTORY
GREEK VICTORY
INDECISIVE

1. Locris   4. Attica
2. Boeotia   5. Phocis
3. Euboea   6. Argolis

0   NAUTICAL MILES   100

ABOVE: *The pass of Thermopylae as it is today. In 480 BC the coastline would have been just to the right of the road.*

FAR RIGHT: *A bust of a Greek soldier. The bronze "Corinthian" helmet would have been pulled forward to protect the face in battle.*

a simple frontal attack, where their comparative lack of armor put them at a grave disadvantage. Even these magnificent troops were repulsed by the disciplined phalanxes, and as night fell, Persian bodies littered the front of the Greek defensive wall with no appreciable gains made. To cap a disastrous day, the Persian fleet had also been roughly handled. A detachment that had been sent round the eastern coast of the long island of Euboea was wrecked by a storm, while a surprise Greek naval attack had caused many casualties at Artemision.

After a night spent resting and tending their wounds, both sides renewed the hard and bitter struggle at daybreak, with men hacking and stabbing at each other in the fierce August heat. By the end of this second long day, the Greek line remained unbroken, although every man knew that defeat was only a matter of time. Sheer weight of numbers would inevitably wear them down, but Leonidas was determined to hold the pass for as long as possible.

By now the Persians were also looking for an inland route to bypass the Greeks, but lack of local knowledge would have hindered this. The

mountain tracks that existed were narrow, winding and rocky, and to send large bodies of heavily armed troops into the hills with no idea of where they would end up would have been folly. The solution was at hand, however, in the shape of a renegade Greek named Ephialtes. He informed the Persian king that he knew of a route through the hills, one which would bring a force of soldiers round behind the defenders. The Immortals were the ideal force for such a mission, well experienced in mobile mountain warfare and thirsting for revenge after their disastrous first attack. That night they set off on a silent march, led by Ephialtes.

Aware of the existence of this path, Leonidas had earlier dispatched 1000 Phocians inland as a blocking force, but they seem to have been totally unprepared when the attack came, being easily brushed aside by the Immortals. Messengers must have escaped, for as dawn broke, Leonidas was aware of the fact that he had been outflanked and that his position was doomed. He held a council of war as the sun rose, and accounts differ as to what took place. Some say that he ordered the main part of his army to retreat while the Spartan contingent

ABOVE: *a fifth century BC stone frieze showing Greek Hoplites in combat.*

RIGHT: *Athenian triremes totally outclassed the Persian warships at Artemision and Salamis. Their oars were in three banks, each oar wielded by one man.*

stayed, others say that he asked for volunteers to stay. The Spartans' warrior code left them no option but to stand at their posts, but they were not the only Greeks to remain. They were also joined by the contingents from Thebes and Thespia, making a total force of some 2000 left to face attacks from both the front and rear.

The Persian assaults were soon renewed, and the Greeks fought desperately through the morning, the hoplites gradually falling in savage hand-to-hand combat. Leonidas was killed relatively early, a bitter struggle taking place over his body. As their spears became broken or were wrenched out of their hands, the Greeks resorted to their short swords, stones, or even their bare hands. Eventually, the full power of the Immortals' assault made itself felt, and the survivors pulled back to a small, rocky mound to make their last stand. Some of the Thebans felt that they had fought enough, and surrendered, but the men from Sparta remained true to their code, and with their allies from Thespia, they prepared to fight and die. In the final minutes the Persians attacked with arrows, spears and other missiles before overwhelming the few remaining defenders in a last deadly rush.

The military effect of the Spartan sacrifice was negligible – the Persian host soon continued its inexorable march south, ravaging the peninsula and sacking major Greek cities on its way. The effects on morale were much more important, however. The example of the Spartans and their allies acted as a beacon to the other Greek states, encouraging unity and eventual victory over the invaders. The last stand also had a deep effect on the minds of the Persians, demonstrating that they were in the midst of hostile peoples who would fight hard and die in defense of their freedom. When a few months later, after a naval defeat at Salamis, Xerxes retreated the majority of his army back to Persia, the memory of the rows of unyielding shields in the narrow mountain pass at Thermopylae must have had a powerful influence on his final decision.

RIGHT: The Persian "Immortals" were lightly armored shock troops, armed with a curved bow and long stabbing spear.

Acre
1191

"As long as our enemies are hastening hither by sea and land, our country is threatened by the greatest disasters . . ."

SALADIN

BELOW: Most of the surviving defenses of Acre date from the nineteenth century, but sections of the medieval walls can still be seen.

IN 1187 THE Frankish Crusader state of Jerusalem had been overrun, with the battered remnants of the Christian army holed up in the coastal town of Tyre. The army of Salah ad-Din Yusuf (known as Saladin in the west) had destroyed that of King Guy of Jerusalem at the Battle of Hattin, and the cities of Acre and Jerusalem had fallen soon after. Guy and many of his senior knights had been taken prisoner, so the defense of Tyre fell on the shoulders of his great rival, Conrad of Montferrat.

Saladin was a clever politician as well as a soldier, so he released Guy and many other prisoners in the hope that the arguments and dissensions that had already weakened the Franks would continue. He was proven right when Conrad refused to acknowledge Guy as his King, keeping him outside the walls of Tyre. In August 1189, in a desperate attempt to regain his kingdom, Guy took as many soldiers as he could muster and marched on Acre, the fortified Crusader city now held by the Moslems. Before being released by Saladin he had vowed never to fight Moslems again, a promise conveniently forgotten in his bid for power.

His few thousand soldiers encamped a few miles outside Acre on 28 August occupying high ground to the east of the city. Acre sits on

the Mediterranean coast of the Holy Land, and was protected at that time by the sea and a high wall to the south and east. The north and west sides had a much stronger stone wall, with high bastions and towers along its length. The Moslem defenders had made good the damage caused when they took the city from the Christians, and had prepared by storing supplies of food, water and armaments in expectation of an attack and siege. The city's harbor was well defended by a long stone wall and tower, and the defenders hoped to be able to receive ships even if the land blockade was complete.

Guy's first attack was launched within a few days of his arrival, and was quickly rebuffed. He then settled down for a long siege while waiting

ABOVE: At Hattin in 1187, Saladin defeated the Christians under King Guy. This manuscript shows him symbolically capturing the "Holy Cross."

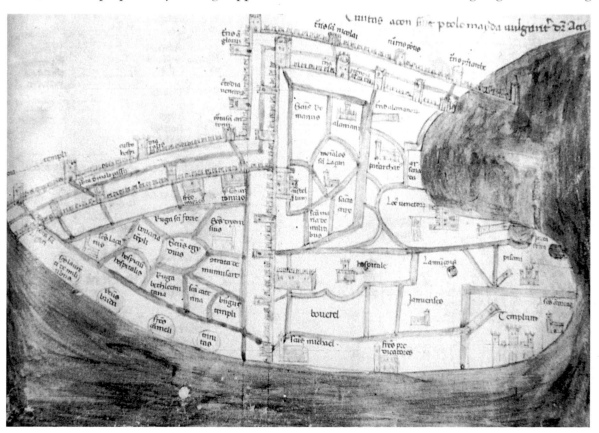

LEFT: Marino Sanudo's plan of Acre dates from the fourteenth century, and shows an outer wall added after the city was recaptured from Saladin.

17

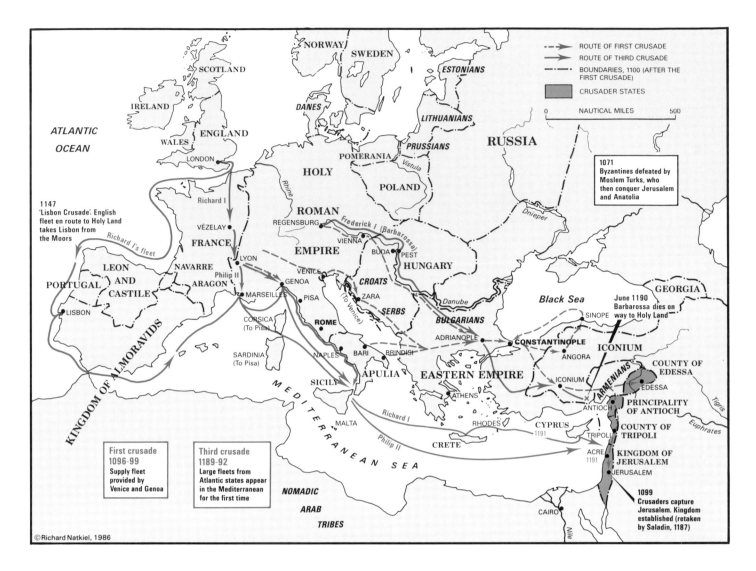

ROUTE OF FIRST CRUSADE
ROUTE OF THIRD CRUSADE
BOUNDARIES, 1100 (AFTER THE FIRST CRUSADE)
CRUSADER STATES

0   NAUTICAL MILES   500

NORWAY
SWEDEN
SCOTLAND
ESTONIANS
IRELAND
DANES
LITHUANIANS
WALES   ENGLAND
PRUSSIANS   RUSSIA
ATLANTIC OCEAN
LONDON
POMERANIA
Vistula
HOLY
POLAND
Rhine
ROMAN
1147
'Lisbon Crusade'. English fleet en route to Holy Land takes Lisbon from the Moors
Richard I
REGENSBURG   Frederick I (Barbarossa)
EMPIRE
Richard I's fleet
VÉZELAY   VIENNA
Dnieper
LEON   LYON   BUDA   PEST
NAVARRE   Philip II   VENICE   HUNGARY
PORTUGAL   AND   ARAGON   GENOA   CROATS   Danube   GEORGIA
CASTILE   MARSEILLES   PISA   (To Venice)   ZARA   Black Sea   June 1190 Barbarossa dies on way to Holy Land
LISBON   SERBS
1071
Byzantines defeated by Moslem Turks, who then conquer Jerusalem and Anatolia
CORSICA (To Pisa)   ROME   BULGARIANS   SINOPE
ADRIANOPLE   CONSTANTINOPLE   ICONIUM
SARDINIA (To Pisa)   NAPLES   BARI   BRINDISI   ANGORA
KINGDOM OF ALMORAVIDS   SICILY   APULIA   EASTERN EMPIRE   ICONIUM
ARMENIANS   COUNTY OF EDESSA
MEDITERRANEAN   ATHENS   ANTIOCH   EDESSA   Tigris
Richard I   PRINCIPALITY OF ANTIOCH
MALTA   RHODES   CYPRUS   Euphrates
Philip II   1191   TRIPOLI   COUNTY OF TRIPOLI
CRETE   SEA   ACRE   KINGDOM OF JERUSALEM
1191
JERUSALEM
NOMADIC
First crusade 1096-99 Supply fleet provided by Venice and Genoa   Third crusade 1189-92 Large fleets from Atlantic states appear in the Mediterranean for the first time
ARAB   CAIRO   1099 Crusaders capture Jerusalem. Kingdom established (retaken by Saladin, 1187)
TRIBES   Nile
©Richard Natkiel, 1986

ABOVE: The Crusades were one of the most colorful episodes in European and Middle Eastern history. Richard's 3rd Crusade was one of the better-organized campaigns.

RIGHT: A fourteenth century illuminated manuscript showing Saladin and Moslem horsemen.

for reinforcements from Europe. Saladin meanwhile gathered such troops that he could, leading them into an attack on the Christian army on 15 September. He was too weak to push them out of their camp, so he contented himself with cutting off their land communications and settling down to besiege the besiegers. Through that winter, both sides launched numerous attacks on each other with little success, and after a time the armies settled down to a pattern of fraternization when not actually engaged in combat.

Small groups of reinforcements arrived to add to Guy's strength, including Danes, Spaniards, Flemings, and Sicilians. At first, Moslem supply vessels were also able to sail into and out of Acre, but as Guy's ships tightened their grip, this became more and more difficult. The summer passed in stalemate, with famine and disease claiming many, whether inside the city, in the Frankish camp, or in Saladin's lines. Both sides hoped for more reinforcements. Saladin waited for support from the many small Moslem states in the Middle East, while Guy could do little except anticipate the Crusade promised from Europe.

The Crusaders did eventually come, although nearly three years passed after hearing the news of Hattin before the French and English Kings set sail. England and France had been fighting for most of this time, only agreeing to peace after Richard I inherited the English throne from his father Henry II in 1189. Richard, commonly known as "Coeur de Lion," then spent some time consolidating his kingdom, before setting off on his great Crusade in the spring of 1190. Philip Augustus of France set off at the same time, and, a year earlier, a German Crusade under the elderly Emperor Frederick Barbarossa had begun its march through central Europe. However, the Emperor's death in an accident caused his army to disintegrate in chaos, and only a few disorganized remnants actually reached the city of Acre.

On 20 April 1191, King Philip landed near Acre, his men providing a much-needed boost to the siege. His cousin Conrad had earlier

ABOVE RIGHT: The preserved mail suit and helmet of a Moslem warrior of the period.

RIGHT: Richard I of England and Philip II of France provided the backbone of the 3rd Crusade, launched to reclaim the Holy Land.

ABOVE: *A fourteenth century view of crusaders besieging a castle. A simple trebuchet stone-thrower can be seen.*

RIGHT: *Horses were used in combat by both sides, although the crusader cavalry were usually better armored than their Moslem opponents.*

come to a reluctant agreement with Guy, co-operating with the siege and organizing the delivery of supplies from Tyre; but Philip's arrival saw another burst of intrigue and maneuvering. Richard had meanwhile found time to sack Messina en route, and at that time was harbored in Cyprus, where he had already been angered by the conduct of the self-styled Emperor Isaac. Here he met King Guy, who had sailed from the battlefront to plead his case. Richard persuaded Guy that Cyprus could be a vital strategic asset in the Mediterranean, so the armies of the two men launched a quick invasion which ended in the defeat of Isaac and the marriage of the Emperor's daughter to Richard.

It was nearly four years after Hattin when Richard and his soldiers finally reached the Holy Land, landing seven weeks after Philip on 8 June 1191. This energetic and dynamic warrior quickly put new energy into the Christians. Massive new siege engines constructed under the aegis of Philip had already been bombarding the walls with heavy stone projectiles, and with the extra reinforcements supplied by Richard renewed pressure was brought to bear on the defenders. Stones would be catapulted on to the walls, and whenever a breach appeared an attack would be launched. Saladin's army, while weak from hunger and sickness, was still able to pose a threat, and would itself attack whenever the Crusaders assaulted the city, causing them to pull back and defend their camp.

Nevertheless, starvation was rife in the city and the unpalatable truth of defeat was staring the defenders in the face. On 4 July they sent envoys to the Crusader camp to ask for terms, but were turned away. Saladin heard of this, and tried to make one more attack on the Christians the next day, but his army was too weak from fatigue and hunger. On the 11th, the city capitulated, in a deal which involved Saladin having to pay an indemnity of 200,000 gold pieces and releasing 1500 Christian prisoners. The Crusaders would have the city and all its contents, but the defenders would all be released unharmed.

Shocked by this surrender, Saladin nevertheless felt obliged to honor the agreement. While the Crusaders took their newly-won prize, bickering among themselves over the spoils, he gathered the men and money needed to pay this debt, sending the first installment one month later. He sent the correct amount of money, but some of the prisoners specifically

named in the agreement were not among those released. Richard was by now impatient to be on the move, and so, using the fact that Saladin had failed to release all of the prisoners that had been requested as an excuse, he ordered his 2700 prisoners from the city to be put to the sword. In an act of peculiarly cold-blooded brutality his troops enthusiastically hacked their way through the mass of prisoners, who included the families of some of the Moslem soldiers.

Richard then set off toward Jerusalem, his army shadowed by that of Saladin. A short campaign followed, ending in a Christian victory of sorts, and most of the Holy Land was eventually recaptured for the Cross. However, the Crusaders never managed to recapture their most prized objective, the city of Jerusalem, and their campaign must be regarded, in essence, as a failure. Their capital would remain in Acre, until the army of al-Ashraf finally removed the Crusaders for good in 1291.

ABOVE: A rather stylized view of the siege which contains a number of inaccuracies in both armor and weaponry. For example, the Crusaders would not have used longbows.

Calais

1347

"I can no longer behold my fellow citizens dying of hunger. I have hope of God's mercy if I must die to save the people; and I offer myself to go on this mission for their sake."

EUSTACE DE ST. PIERRE

IN AUGUST 1346 the French army had been devastated at Crécy, leaving the English free to rampage around northeast France. King Edward III's archers had just won their spectacular victory in his attempt to win the French crown, although his army was now too weak to take much advantage of this. However, the English King was not yet ready to take his men home. Paris may have been out of reach, but the port of Calais was a tempting target; a fortified town just 25 miles over the English Channel from Dover, whose capture would provide excellent access to Flanders and a springboard for future adventures in France. So in late August 1346 his army of 12–15,000 soldiers marched northward, arriving outside the walls of Calais by 9 September.

Calais in 1346 was a small town of some 5000 inhabitants, relying on sea trade with the rest of Europe for its prosperity. Its harbor was well protected by a stone wall, while double stone walls separated by a flooded moat surrounded the land boundaries of the town. Much of the surrounding countryside was wet marsh – terrain which would hamper the deployment of a besieging army and prevent tunnels being dug to undermine the walls. The governor was a man called John de Vienne, a Burgundian who was determined to hold out as long as possible. His first action was typical of the grim rules of a medieval siege, in that he banished some 2000 women, children and elderly from the town; "useless mouths" of no military value. These unfortunates were allowed to pass through the English lines after being given a little food.

Not having sufficient strength to take the town by storm, the English settled down to a long siege. King Edward sent for supplies and reinforcements from England, including the primitive siege artillery kept in the Tower of London. His camp soon took on an air of permanence, with the wooden buildings constructed to protect the army through the winter

FAR LEFT: *The claims that Edward III of England made on the French crown eventually triggered the bloody conflict known as the Hundred Years War: a series of conflicts which lasted from 1337 to 1453.*

ABOVE: *When the English army pitched camp outside Calais, they had to face a flooded marsh as well as the city walls.*

RIGHT: *A contemporary view of battle outside the city walls.*

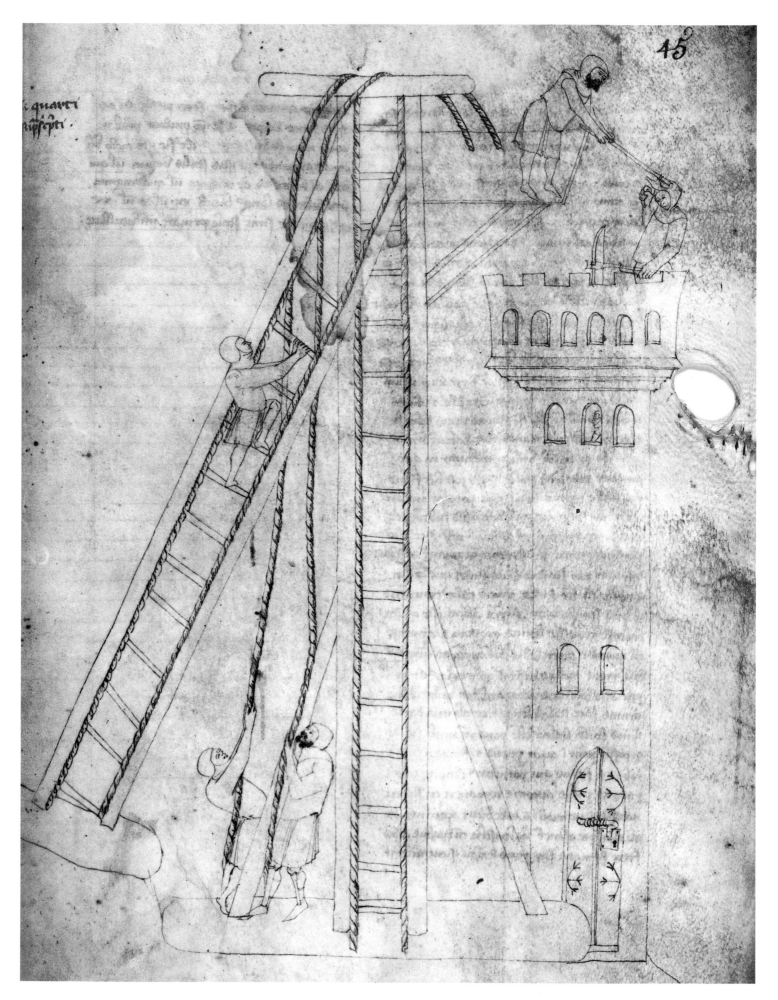

forming a small town which became known as "Newtown The Bold." Flemish traders and landowners were quick to see the opportunity, and a thriving market soon established itself.

The winter months took their toll, however. The dysentry and other diseases that ravaged the army were compounded by shortages of food, and conditions inside the city were even worse as food supplies rapidly diminished. First the cattle, then the horses, then dogs and cats were all eaten, and soon men were turning to such delicacies as boiled or fried rat. Eventually 500 more civilians were thrown out of the city, but this time the English mood was not so chivalrous and they were left to starve in the no-man's land that lay between the walls and the besiegers.

Spring 1347 saw the English army almost in a state of collapse, with thousands dead and the rest sick or fatigued. Edward spurred his government to recruit more troops, and a stream of adventurers and pressed men crossed the Channel seeking glory or fortune. Convicted murderers were even offered the option of serving in the army as an alternative to their sentence. As the warmer weather approached, the besieging army grew to over 32,000, composed mostly of new men who had not suffered the debilitating effects of the winter.

There was little respite inside the walls however, apart from the occasional supply ship that managed to run the English blockade. De Vienne sent frantic messages to King Philip of France asking for help, and one of these was intercepted by the English, who in a moment of sublime confidence passed it on to the intended recipient. In it the plight of the town was made clear, "we have nothing left to subsist on, unless we eat each other."

Philip was having great difficulty in raising a new army after the Crécy disaster. Many were reluctant to serve, while his States General initially refused to provide more money for what could be another debacle. In July, the Duke of Burgundy eventually attempted an attack along the coast, but his relief force was stopped near Boulogne by Flemish allies of Edward. Burgundy withdrew to Sangatte where his king had finally appeared with a relieving army. The French and English troops spent the next few days glowering at each other, fighting the occasional skirmish and duel while challenges were issued and negotiations took place. Philip had little stomach for the fight, and after a few days the desperate men watching from the walls of Calais were horrified to see their rescuers pack their tents and move off without giving battle.

De Vienne realized that despite their stubborn defense, the city was lost, and that surrender was now his only option. His first request for terms was turned down, but one of Edward's senior advisers, Sir Walter de Manny, persuaded the King of the long-term advantages of being seen as a chivalrous conqueror. Edward's final offer to de Vienne was still a grim one – six prominent burghers should be led before him in chains, bearing the keys to the town. Once they had been executed the rest of the defenders could leave unmolested. De Vienne could do nothing but hold a meeting with the horrified defenders and explain the terms. The men stood in silence until one of the wealthiest, Eustace de St Pierre, came forward to volunteer, crying that he could watch his neighbors starve no longer. Five more followed his example and they were soon led by de Vienne through the city gates, dressed in sackcloth and wearing halters.

FAR LEFT: Siege towers were often constructed to give the attackers a chance to climb over the walls of a city or castle.

BELOW: Chain mail was still used extensively at this time, although plate armor was becoming more common, especially for men-at-arms.

RIGHT: *Heraldry fulfilled a vital function on the battlefield, being used to identify individual knights and commanders. This is the shield of Edward Plantaganet, the "Black Prince."*

BELOW: *Wearing sackcloth and halters, the six burghers of Calais were led out to Edward III to be executed.*

FAR RIGHT: *Edward Plantaganet was at his father's side during the siege of Calais, and in later years led numerous raids into France.*

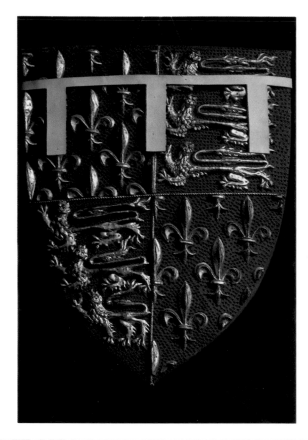

They came before Edward, making a last plea for their lives. As he was giving the order for their execution, Queen Philippa is said to have fallen on her knees, tearfully pleading for him to spare the six. At this Edward relented, and the men were led away. This incident has traditionally been held up as proof of Edward's chivalrous nature, although some historians have claimed that it was deliberately stage-managed to give that precise impression. Whether or not their execution really was intended, the six burghers of Calais have gone down in history as men willing to sacrifice themselves for their comrades, and are commemorated to this day by a fine statue by Rodin.

On 4 August 1347, after a siege lasting almost a year, the English finally took control of the town, ejecting virtually all of the inhabitants and soon populating it with English settlers and merchants. Calais quickly became a valuable *entrepôt* for trade with Flanders, and for over 200 years this town remained an English foothold on the continent of Europe.

Agincourt
1415

"Sirs and fellows, as I am true knight and king, for me this day shall never England ransom pay."

KING HENRY V

IN 1415, THE young, charismatic King Henry V of England had been on the throne for only two years, but he already felt sufficiently strong to attempt the recapture of his family's traditional lands in Aquitaine and Normandy, and perhaps even the French crown. A dynamic soldier with extensive military experience, he had persuaded, cajoled and ordered his leading nobles to prepare for a war, borrowing large sums of money to pay for his expedition. The invasion force that finally set sail from the south of England comprised some 2500 men-at-arms, about 8000 archers, and over 1000 gunners, surgeons, carpenters, fletchers, blacksmiths, bakers and other essential elements of a medieval army.

The military elite were the men-at-arms, soldiers of noble birth who fought encased in over 80 pounds of armor and tended to regard war as an honorable contest between men of valor and breeding. By the early fifteenth

BELOW: By 1415, a knight's armor was almost completely made from steel plate. This preserved specimen shows the cuisse, poleyn and grieve used to protect the leg and knee.

century, their armor was almost exclusively of steel plate, with the wearer being protected from head to foot from all but direct heavy blows or lunges with metal tipped spears against the joints, visor and other weak points. Armed with a large sword or heavy ax, he normally rode into battle on horseback and dismounted to fight. In most respects, the training and equipment of the English man-at-arms was similar to that of his French opponent, as was his social standing and background.

The mass of the English army was not provided by noble knights, however, but by archers of less exalted birth. Henry's army had nearly 8000 bowmen, nearly half of whom rode on horseback. They were lightly protected, wearing jerkins made from leather, sometimes with steel strips as reinforcement, and with a simple leather or steel cap. The archer's weapon was the Welsh longbow, made from six feet of yew, elm or ash, and able to shoot effec-

tively at up to 400 yards. A skilled man had a good chance of a kill at approximately half that distance, and with specially-shaped arrowheads he could penetrate armor at around 60 yards. He also carried a sword, short ax or a dagger for self-defense.

On 18 August 1415, the English landed at Harfleur, a coastal port at the mouth of the Seine which would act as a secure base and allow access to Normandy. Protected by stone walls, flooded ditches and swampland, the tiny garrison held out for six weeks; a costly delay to Henry. The weather was worsening, large quantities of supplies had been consumed, and the scourge of dysentry had swept through the army, killing nearly 2000, incapacitating 2000 or so more, and weakening many of the remainder. Morale was not improved by Henry's strict orders forbidding the looting and pillaging of Harfleur and the surrounding countryside, which would normally be regarded as the rightful privilege of the victorious soldier. As Henry was supposed to be liberating his own land and property, he could hardly allow his army to strip the country bare and kill or rape the population.

Henry realized that his army was now too weak to undertake the planned march on Paris, but honor demanded a demonstration of force and authority; so he decided to march the 6000 men still fit to fight up the coast to the English enclave of Calais, setting off on 8 October. Speed of movement was essential, so the majority of the heavy equipment, baggage, siege artillery and supplies were left behind. Each man carried his weapons and one week's rations, with packhorses carrying the armor and shields of the men-at-arms.

Personal and dynastic rivalries among the French court, combined with a sick and weak king had prevented a strong, co-ordinated response, although theoretically the strength available was many times larger than the English force. King Charles VI was subject to bouts of mental illness and insanity, so he was unfit to lead the armies himself. Rivalries between the Dukes of Burgundy and Orleans prevented command being given to either of those senior nobles, and in the end a compromise was sought. Two highly experienced soldiers, Charles d'Albret, the Constable of France, and Boucicault, the Marshal, were asked to lead the French forces, under the nominal command of Louis, the Dauphin. Boucicault and d'Albret were skilled soldiers, but lacked the social rank necessary to control the quarrelsome and arro-

gant French nobility. The lack of a single, strong leader respected by all would be a major factor in the disaster that was to follow.

An advance guard of some 6000 men under d'Albret had formed up at Honfleur; the Marshal was with another force at Rouen; while the Dauphin was with the main body at Vernon. The French commanders were reluctant to face the English in pitched battle, and instead chose to shadow and contain the enemy, letting disease, hunger and fatigue do their work. For five days the English moved up the coast, obtaining food supplies by threats and intimidation, and by 13 October, they were approaching the only significant obstacle on their route, the Somme river. As they came within a few miles of their planned crossing point at Blanchetacque, a prisoner revealed the shocking news that the ford was blocked by French forces, while d'Albret and his advance guard had made a rapid march to Abbeville and now controlled the river farther inland. Food was running short; sickness and fatigue were rife; the autumn weather was cold and wet, and the army was still some 50 miles from safety. The

ABOVE: *It was to be nearly 40 years after his father's army was defeated at Agincourt before Charles VII finally drove the English out of France.*

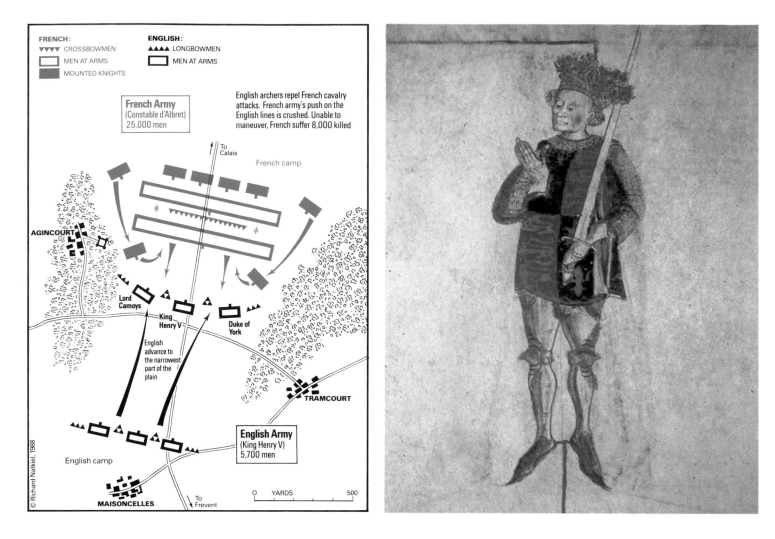

FRENCH:
▼▼▼▼ CROSSBOWMEN
☐ MEN AT ARMS
■ MOUNTED KNIGHTS

ENGLISH:
▲▲▲▲ LONGBOWMEN
☐ MEN AT ARMS

French Army
(Constable d'Albret)
25,000 men

English archers repel French cavalry attacks. French army's push on the English lines is crushed. Unable to maneuver, French suffer 8,000 killed

To Calais

French camp

AGINCOURT

Lord Camoys

King Henry V

Duke of York

English advance to the narrowest part of the plain

TRAMCOURT

English Army
(King Henry V)
5,700 men

English camp

MAISONCELLES

To Frevent

0   YARDS   500

© Richard Natkiel, 1988

ABOVE: The French army deployed in the narrow gap between the woods of Tramcourt and Agincourt, thus negating the advantage of their superior numbers.

ABOVE RIGHT: King Henry V in plate armor, wearing no helmet but with his coat of arms and sword.

road ahead was well and truly blocked, and the only solution was to follow the course of the Somme inland to try and find an unguarded crossing point, even if this meant moving farther away from Calais.

Thus the English turned to the southeast, with the French shadowing them from across the river. The French main body was also on the move, and by the 17th it had crossed the river at Amiens and was moving to Bapaume. To the English, the situation must have had the makings of a first-class catastrophe. Herded inland, with little information on the river and countryside, they were dancing to the enemy's tune in the knowledge that the road home was blocked.

From Fouilly, the Somme curves to the northeast to Peronne then back south to Voyennes. When he reached this point, Henry decided to cut across the base of this loop, to Chaunnes and Nesle. The French would have to travel a much longer distance on the north bank, which might give the English enough time to find a crossing before they could react. On the 18th, the army reached Nesle, and the local peasants, understandably anxious to see

the back of 6000 starving men and their horses, told the English of unguarded fords nearby at Voyennes and Bethencourt. Early the next day, the weary army found two narrow causeways across the Somme, and after a few hours repair work, they passed across the river without any serious interference.

The English now had nearly 100 miles to travel, but at least the road was open and they were marching in the right direction. Over the next few days, they were shadowed by the French as they moved north, and on the 24th, the first sighting of the enemy's main force was made when Henry's soldiers saw the way ahead blocked by three immense columns of men. That night the French encamped behind the woods at Tramcourt and astride the road to Calais. As Henry moved his army into billets around the village of Maisoncelles, none had doubts that tomorrow they would have to fight. The next day, 25 October, would be the Feast of St. Crispin, a comforting thought to those who believed that God was on their side. It was about the only comfort for the English that night, as they prepared to meet a force over six times their own strength. Most had eaten nothing but a few nuts and berries for the last few days, many were suffering from dysentry, and all were cold, exhausted and soaked by the constant rain. Battle could no longer be avoided – the only way home was through the French army.

As dawn broke, the weaknesses of the messy and vague French command structure became apparent, however, as their army deployed in a position guaranteed to rob them of most of the advantages of superior numbers. The forest of Tramcourt hemmed in the French left flank, while the woods around Agincourt village fixed the positions of their right. The width of the battlefield at this point was only some 1300 yards, which was insufficient space to array the large numbers of Frenchmen. This position left a frontal assault against the English front line as the only tactical option for both the foot soldiers and the cavalry. D'Albret and Bouc-icault were well aware of the disadvantages of such a deployment, but by this time they had lost any meaningful control over their quar-relsome and arrogant feudal superiors.

BELOW: A contemporary view of the later battle at Patay shows the armored cavalry of the period fighting with sword and lance.

The French front division or "battle" comprised some 8000 dismounted men-at-arms arrayed six deep, with some 2400 heavy cavalry on the flanks. Behind it the second "battle" consisted of some 4000 to 6000 men-at-arms and crossbowmen, with about 8000 to 10,000 mounted men-at-arms, pages and servants farther to the rear in the third "battle." The English deployed their 1000 men-at-arms in a field of young corn, in three groups from right to left, arrayed three or four men deep. The bulk of their 5000 archers were placed on the flanks, angled slightly forward to fire into the center. Sources also talk of triangular wedges of archers between the men-at-arms, but such a formation must have weakened the line.

For much of the morning the two armies faced each other, separated by 1200 yards of rain-soaked ground. During this time, the lack of discipline in the French army had its effect, as knights wandered out of position to relieve boredom, talk to friends, make peace with enemies, and generally make a social outing of the whole affair. Some in the second and third ranks jostled their way to the front, bundling the archers and crossbowmen to the rear and further increasing the congestion in the front lines of the French army.

Meanwhile, the English hope that they could draw a French attack on to them was fading. The final exhortations to the troops had been made and the only thing left to do was to advance and force the battle. Around midday, Henry ordered the army forward. Careful not to exhaust his men and lose formation in the sodden, slippery ground, he led them in a slow, steady march, until they were within about 300 yards of the enemy front line. Once the order to stop was given, the archers hammered and drove sharpened, six-foot, wooden stakes into the ground. Designed to protect them from cavalry charges, these heavy stakes had been carried by the tired men for over a week, and they were no doubt glad to be free of them.

Once the archers were prepared, the first massed salvos of arrows shot into the air, finally stinging the French army into action, with their crossbowmen firing one or two shots then hastily retiring. The French attack started when the cavalry on each flank was ordered forward against the English archers. The heavy warhorses moved forward, churning the wet ground into a muddy morass, their hooves slipping and sliding on the trampled grass and corn. The armor of the riders protected most of them from the archers' fire, but the dense formations soon became totally disrupted as arrows bit into the unprotected flanks and necks of the horses, maddening them into a shrieking panic. In the chaos, only a few attackers actually reached the English lines, where they ran into the sharp forest of defensive stakes. By this time the rest of the cavalry were in confused retreat.

In the meantime, the French first division had been given the order to attack, and the armored men were struggling forward through the churned ground. This formation was totally devastated by the mass of horsemen crashing back through their midst, reducing what was supposed to be a compact armored fist into disorganized rabble. Nevertheless, the cream of the French aristocracy struggled and slipped through the mud to get to grips with their opponents. Hard and bloody hand-to-hand fighting began, with men swinging massive, heavy axes and swords against each other, attempting to chop through armor, flesh and bone in a brutal contest. As more of the French pushed forward behind their leaders, the crush of so many men in a restricted space impacted on their own front line, knocking some to the ground and preventing others from swinging or even drawing their weapons.

BELOW: English archers were lightly protected, but their massed salvos and rapid rate of fire completely devastated the French cavalry.

It was as this desperate combat was taking place that the English archers dropped their bows and swept around behind the French knights, chopping and stabbing at the joints and weak points of their armor. Such an action was a shocking surprise to most of the French nobility, who regarded such lowly-born men as irrelevant sword fodder. The lightly protected archers were able to move quickly in the mud and rain, nimble enough to dodge most of the clumsy blows from the encumbered and visored men. It was this attack that finished the French knights, turning a battle into a slaughter.

ABOVE: A contemporary view of the Battle of Agincourt showing details of weapons, armor and equipment.

33

Once the unfolding disaster became apparent, the much weaker French second division was launched into the attack, adding to the chaos of the slaughter and being dispatched in the same way as their predecessors. The third division could only sit and watch in horror, some taking the opportunity to slip away into the countryside.

During the afternoon, the English tended their wounded and scavenged the battlefield for valuable weapons, equipment and armor, until a dangerous new threat appeared. Some of the third French division had been rallied, and 600 mounted knights were preparing to attack. At around the same time, reports reached Henry of an attack by a mixed force of peasants and men-at-arms on the English rear, which was destroying baggage and supplies. These attacks seemed to be part of a co-ordinated plan and for a few moments posed a great worry to the English king. Some 1500 valuable high-ranking French prisoners were being held, and rather than risk them being freed by their compatriots, Henry gave the notorious order to have them executed. In the event both French attacks were quickly dealt with and the execution order rescinded, although not before

a good number of the prisoners were killed by their guards.

As dusk fell, the victors withdrew to Maisoncelles, taking as much booty and captured food as they could carry. His battered army too weak to exploit the victory, Henry led them along the open road to Calais, finally returning to Dover on 16 November. The French elite classes had been decimated, with between 6000 and 10,000 dead – around 600 of those from the most senior families in the land. English casualties were minimal, although stories of less than 100 dead were largely propaganda, and a figure of just under 500 is more likely.

While no major strategic gains had been made, the capture of Harfleur gave a good base for successful future campaigns in Normandy, after which Henry sealed his succession to the French throne by marrying Charles' daughter in 1420. In a final twist of irony, he never lived to claim this inheritance, dying of an illness in 1422. He was followed to the grave by his father-in-law only two months later. The joint crown of England and France would be held by Henry's baby son, although within another 30 years or so the vast majority of the English possessions in France would be lost for ever.

BELOW: This fifteenth century view of the battle is incorrect in that it shows identical deployment on both sides. The French did not have great numbers of archers, while the English army formed up in one line.

Constantinople
1453

"Only one thing I want: Give me Constantinople!"

SULTAN MEHMET II

BY 1453 CONSTANTINOPLE WAS a decaying shadow of its former self, as was the Byzantine empire ruled from this once great city on the Bosphorus. The new emperor, Constantine XI, was a skilled and respected soldier and administrator, but even he was unable to prevent religious schism with the west and continuing encroachment from the east. His most implacable enemy was the Ottoman Sultan, Mehmet II (sometimes known as Mohammed II), a young man determined to finally reduce the city which had been such an obstacle to the expansion of his father's empire. Within one year of his accession in 1451, his castle on the east side of the Bosphorus was able to control naval access to the city, and by April 1453, he and his troops were encamped outside Constantinople's walls.

The city was situated on a roughly triangular peninsula, bound in the northeast by the waters of the Golden Horn and to the south and east by the Sea of Marmara. It was protected from seaborne attack by a single wall and the dangerous currents that swept its rocky coastline, supplemented by a strong chain, or boom, stretched on floats across the mouth of the Golden Horn. The land side was protected by some of the most elaborate fortifications yet seen on any city, a formidable 400-year-old complex of walls, towers and ditches. The outer obstacle was a deep ditch or foss, of around 60 feet in width and which could be flooded in some sections. Inside this were two high stone walls, each with fortified towers built at intervals along their length. Manning these walls would be a problem, however, as the population of less than 100,000 could only muster around 5000 fighting men, while various foreign contingents of mercenaries and volunteers provided another 2000. The most respected of these was a group of 700 Genoese led by the experienced soldier Giovanni Giustiniani Longo.

The Emperor and Giustiniani deployed the majority of their troops on the land fortifications, but even so, only the outer wall could be fully manned. The sea walls had to be left lightly guarded, with great reliance placed on the boom and the ships protecting it. One saving grace was that the defenders were well equipped with armor and armed with swords,

ABOVE: Known as "The Conqueror," Sultan Mehmet II was a clever and able leader who greatly increased the power and extent of the Ottoman Empire.

LEFT: *The desperate attempts of the Turkish assault troops to scale the city walls.*

ABOVE: *Once the Turks had breached the walls, they swept through the city, killing, burning and looting.*

BELOW: *A view of the land defenses, showing the double walls.*

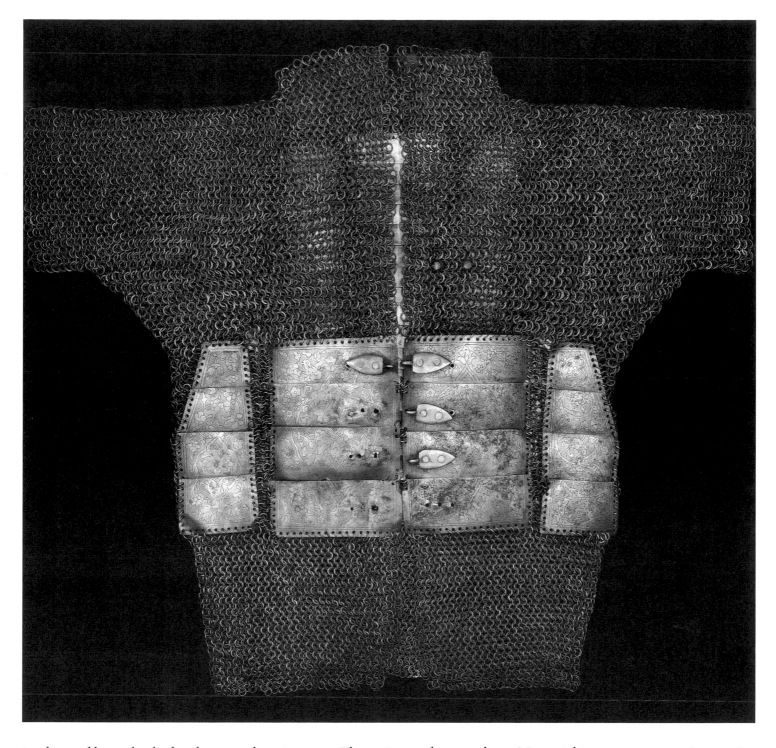

javelins and bows, backed up by stone throwing mangonels and a few cannon. Outside massed some 80,000 regular Turkish troops plus 20,000 bashi-bazouks, irregulars from all corners of Mehmet's empire. The elite were the Janissary Guard, a warrior caste formed from men of Christian origin but who had been brought up from childhood in the Moslem faith and who lived and trained as dedicated professional soldiers. The Sultan had also created an artillery train more powerful than any seen in battle before. Twelve massive siege guns would batter the stone walls to fragments, supplemented by over 50 smaller cannon.

The main attack was to be at Mesoteichion, where the land walls crossed the valley of the River Lycus. The Janissaries had been arrayed there along with the largest guns, and behind could be seen the banners and tents of the Sultan and his court. To support this army, over 120 ships had also been assembled in the Bosphorus. As this mighty force tightened the noose around his city, Constantine sent requests for help from the western world, especially to Rome, Venice and Genoa. None came.

Mehmet opened his attack on 6 April, by pounding the defenses with his guns. By the 18th, great chunks had been torn out of the

ABOVE: A chain mail shirt with extra "fish scale" protection around the center of the chest, typical of the Turkish armor of the period.

37

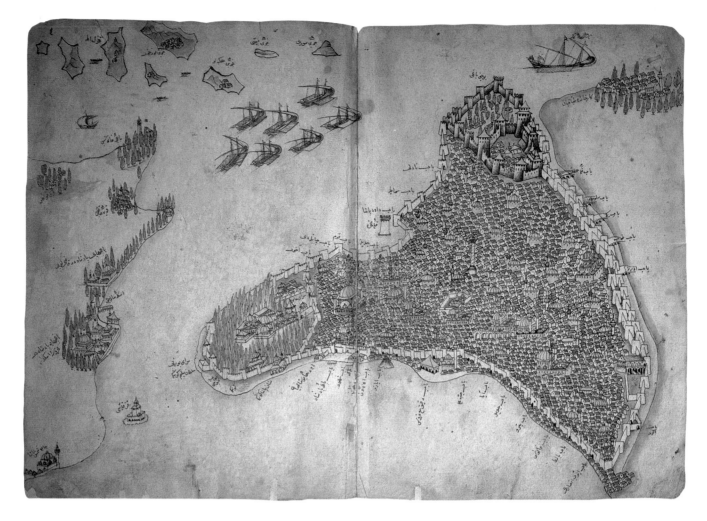

ABOVE: A Turkish manuscript showing a plan of the city. Mehmet's main attack was approximately in the center of the land walls, where they crossed the valley of the River Lycus.

outer walls, although the defenders had managed to repair the gaps with a stockade of wood and earth-filled barrels. That night the Janissaries made the first assault on the walls, but were easily repulsed with over 200 casualties.

The Sultan by now was in a grim humor – his army had failed to make any real impression on the city, while his navy had been humiliated by its inability to pass the boom and its failure to stop supply vessels reaching the defenders. Some new tactic was needed to swing the balance in his favor, and by mid-April his men were working on a timber roadway from the Bosphorus to the north coast of the Golden Horn, skirting the studiously neutral Venetian colony at Pera. On the afternoon of the 22nd, the Greeks were horrified to see a strange procession of ships passing over the low ridge down to the Golden Horn, each vessel on a wheeled cradle and pulled by teams of oxen. That night, over 70 Turkish ships were afloat behind the boom and able to threaten the northeast side of the city.

For the next five weeks, the full gamut of siege warfare continued. Artillery pounded the walls while the defenders struggled to plug the breaches. Mines and counter-mines were dug,

siege towers built, and countless vicious skirmishes, raids and minor battles were fought. By the end of May, both sides realized that the critical moments were upon them. On the 27th, the guns fell ominously silent, as Mehmet's army was given the day to rest and prepare before the final attack, while within the walls prayers were said and hymns sung.

At about 0130 hours on 29 May, the assault was unleashed. All along the walls the Turks roared forward, the irregular bashi-bazouks in the lead. Simultaneous attacks were made on the sea walls, more as a diversion than as a serious threat. The main charge was again in the Lycus valley, where the attackers clambered up the rubble and against the stockade manned by the Greeks and Giustiniani's Italians. They fought in the flickering light of torches and flares, with the continual sound of trumpets and cymbals above the yells and screams of battle. As dawn was breaking, the Janissary regiments were finally sent in, crashing into the defenders in their disciplined formations. Hand-to-hand fighting continued for over an hour, until two events took place that finally shattered the defense.

Some Turks noticed that a small sally port in

the wall at Kerkoporta had been left unbarred after a previous skirmish, and nearly fifty men managed to pour through before the defenders could react and seal the gap. Almost simultaneously, Giustiniani was hit in the chest by a culverin shot. Although the Emperor pleaded with him to stay at his post, he had his bodyguard carry him through the inner wall and across the city to a Genoese ship. In the fear and confusion, the men with him believed all was lost, and poured back through the inner wall. Their retreat coincided with a Janissary assault which finally breached the stockade, forcing the Greeks back against a ditch and the inner wall. As this desperate combat was taking place, a Turkish flag was seen above the gate at Kerkoporta, causing panic among the rest of the Greeks. The Turks pressed on as the defense crumbled, Constantine and his nobles desperately trying to rally their troops. When it became obvious that the city was lost, the Emperor made the cold-blooded decision that

he would not suffer the ignominy of surrender. Removing all identifying insignia, he plunged into the battle. His body was never found.

Once the defense was broken, the slaughter really began. The ordinary soldier could expect little mercy in such a situation, although some senior commanders were taken captive. The victors flooded into the city, eager to loot and pillage. Churches were sacked, as were any houses that appeared to hold valuables. Anyone who resisted was slaughtered out of hand. The immediate effects on the city were catastrophic, with most of those that had manned the walls being killed, and around 50,000 inhabitants taken as slaves. In the long term, however, a new city would grow out of the skeleton of the old. As the center of the Ottoman empire shifted to the Bosphorus, the first steps in creating a new Turkish capital were taking shape. Byzantium and Constantinople were no longer, but the glories of Istanbul would arise from the rubble.

BELOW: The sixth century Basilica of St Sophia survived the fall of the city, becoming a Mosque, and much later a national monument.

Malta

1565

"We for our part are the chosen soldiers of the Cross, and if Heaven requires the sacrifice of our lives, there can be no better occasion than this."

JEAN PARISOT DE LA VALETTE

THE HOSPITALLER KNIGHTS of St. John of Jerusalem were one of the many Christian military-religious orders that flourished during the early crusades. By 1565 these "warrior monks" were the only major order still intact as an independent force, making a living by preying on the sea routes of the Ottoman Empire from their base on the island of Malta. This organized piracy became such a thorn in the side of the empire that the Sultan, Suleiman I, eventually decided to eliminate the order once and for all. Thus on 18 May, his army of 30,000 men, gathered from all corners of the empire, invaded Malta.

The island they landed on was bare and rocky, with few trees, poor soil and little fresh water. Mdina, the capital, sat on high ground in the center of the island, but the key features

TEM
COSTIT:
A
SVLT:
SOLEIM;

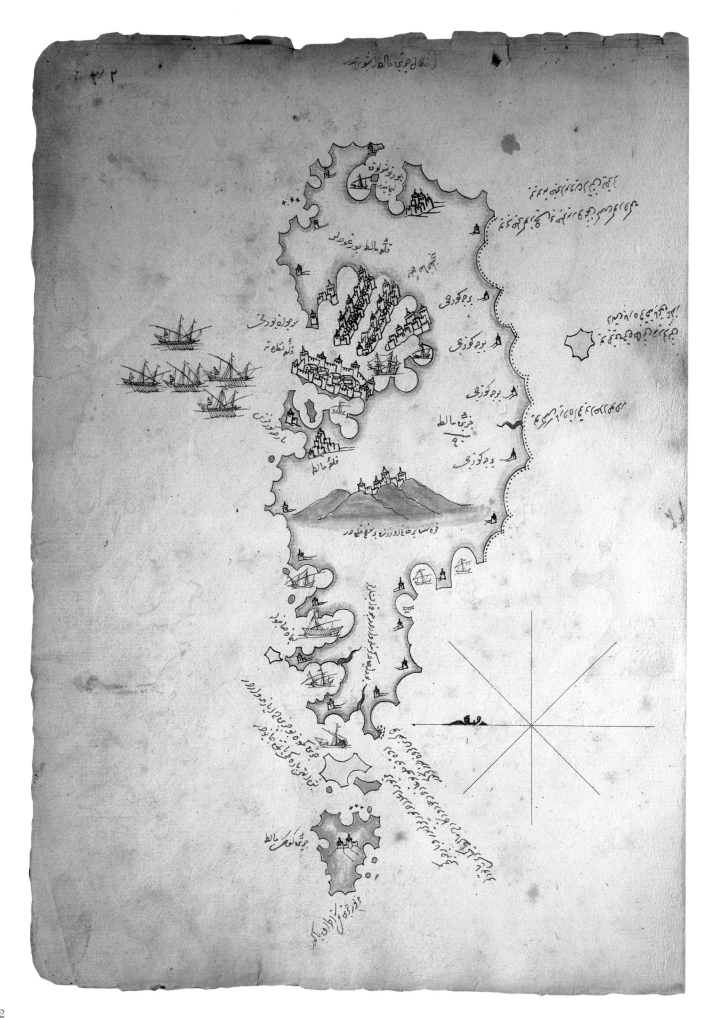

were the two large natural harbors on the east coast, separated by the peninsula of Mt. Sciberras, with the fortress of St. Elmo at its seaward tip. The southern harbor also had two smaller peninsulas jutting into it, the western one holding the fortress of St. Michael and the village of Senglea while the eastern held the town of Birgu and the fort of St. Angelo. Birgu and St. Angelo were where the Hospitallers had their headquarters and most of their religious relics. A wooden pontoon bridge joined both towns, allowing reinforcements to be moved back and forth, and high walls protected both from land and sea attack.

The preparations of the knights had been thorough. The Grand Master of the Order, Jean Parisot de la Valette had carefully planned his defense, ensuring that plenty of food, water, ammunition and powder had been stored. Virtually all of his forces, comprising some 600 knights and about 8000 other soldiers, were in the fortifications of Senglea and Birgu, with a detachment in Fort St. Elmo and the small force of cavalry in Mdina. Most of the non-combatants had been evacuated to Sicily, while the remainder were also behind the walls of the towns.

De la Valette was a determined and powerful man, tempered by a hard life of service to his order. Now 71 years old, he had an iron determination that this bastion of Christendom would not surrender, and that his order would stay on Malta, alive or dead. In contrast, the Turkish expedition had no single strong leader, and suffered from constant bickering between the army and the fleet. Mustapha Pasha, the land commander, wanted to secure Mdina and the rest of the island before tackling the main defenses at Birgu and Fort St. Angelo, but Admiral Piali insisted that Fort Elmo be taken first to allow his 180 ships to use the northernmost harbor. To add to the confusion, the renowned soldier and corsair, Dragut, was also dispatched by the Sultan to "advise" both men.

By 24 May, the Turks had dragged their heavy siege artillery up the rocky hillside of Mt. Sciberras and positioned their troops around Fort St. Elmo. The defenders consisted of some 60 or so knights and 800 soldiers, in a poorly-made sandstone fort overlooked by the high ground of Mt. Sciberras. When the Turkish guns first belched fire and smoke, neither attacker nor defender expected the fort to hold for long. As the cannon balls smashed into the walls, de la Valette realized that the longer the Turks spent against St. Elmo and the

greater their casualties, the weaker they would be when they came to attack the real core of the defense at Birgu. To prolong resistance, he was able to send small groups of reinforcements across the harbor at night, and as long as this lifeline remained open, the fort had a good chance of holding out.

The first major assault was launched in early June, the Turkish troops flooding through the outer defenses against the walls of the fort. In a savage eight-hour battle, the attackers suffered dreadfully from various incendiary devices used by the besieged, including wooden hoops coated in a lethal incendiary composition. These rained down on the Moslems, setting alight their loose robes while entangling their arms and legs, and at the end of the day, some 2000 Turks were dead at a cost of less than 100

ABOVE: The Janissaries were Suleiman's elite shock troops. This image is taken from a sixteenth century Turkish miniature.

FAR LEFT: This Turkish map of the island is drawn with north to the left side of the page, but it shows clearly the main details of the Grand Harbor and its defenses.

Christians. This easy target was proving to be a tougher proposition than at first thought.

The bombardment continued in the ferocious summer heat, gradually demolishing the walls. Even though reinforcements continued to row across the harbor, casualties were rising inexorably. By the end of June the noose had closed completely around the fort, the water crossing from Birgu now made impassable by Turkish fire. On the night of 22 June, the knights in St. Angelo could see the flicker of flames from St. Elmo's chapel as their comrades burnt their religious tapestries and artefacts to prevent desecration by the infidels. They could also hear the mournful toll of the chapel bell sounding a last farewell.

The next day, the massed armies of Mustapha Pasha poured over the rubble of the once proud fortress, overwhelming the last defenders in a no-quarter struggle. The knights fought to the end, including two who had been wounded earlier and who had chairs brought to the walls where they could face their enemies with their swords in their hands. As the battle drew to a close, nine men were taken prisoner – the rest were dead. Over 1500 of the island's de-

ILLVSTRISS. ET. R. F.
IO DE VALLETA, SACRÆ RELIGIONIS HIERO:
SOLIMITANÆ MAGNVS MAGISTER, MELITÆ
INSVLÆ A TVRCIS OBSESSÆ DEFENSOR.
INVICTISS, M·D·LXV.

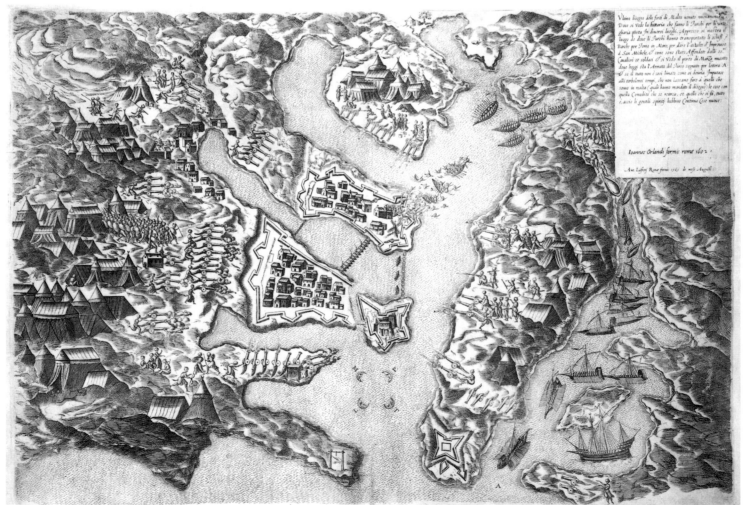

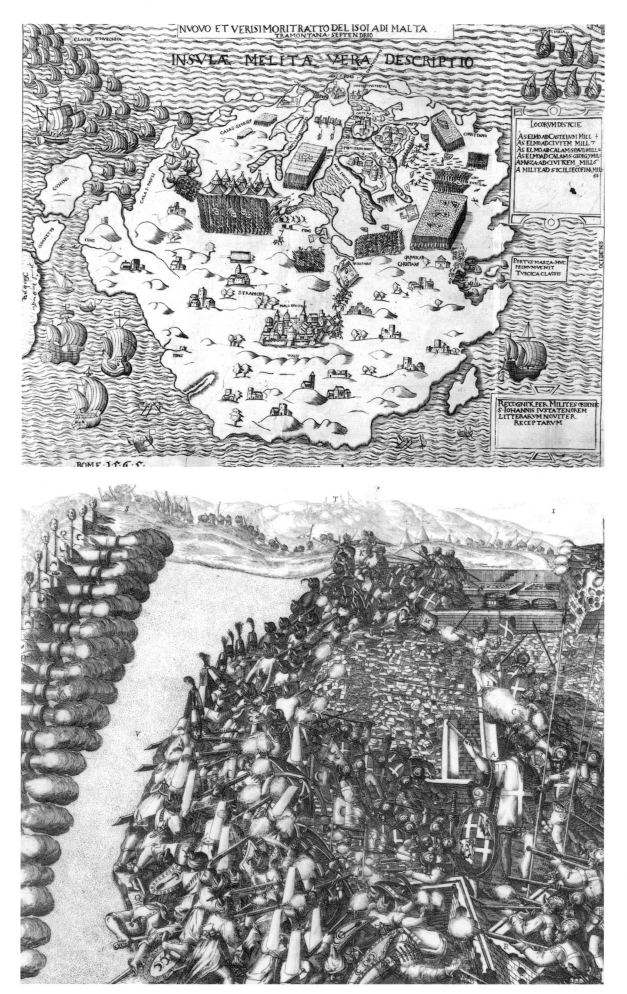

NVOVO ET VERISIMORITRATTO DEL ISOI ADI MALTA
TRAMONTANA SEPTENDRIO

INSVLÆ MELITÆ VERA DESCRIPTIO

LOCORVM DISTICIE
A SELMO AD CASTELVM MILL ½
AS ELMO AD CIVITEM MILL 7
AS ELMO AB CALAM SPAVDI MILL ½
AS ELMO AD CALAM S GEORGY MILL
AMRZA AD CIVI KEM MILLO
A MILITEAD STICILIE COFIN MILL

PORTVS MARZA HVC
PRIMVM VENIT
TVRCICA CLASSIS

RECOGNITK PER MILITES ORDINIS
S IOHANNIS IVSTATENORÆM
LITTERARVM NOVITER
RECEPTARVM

ROME 1565

LEFT: Another plan of the island, this time showing the Christian relief force landing to the right (south) and driving the Turks back to their ships.

LEFT: A crisis was reached in late August, when the Turks managed to breach the walls in a number of places. Each time this happened, de la Valette was able to inspire his men to throw them back and repair the gaps.

45

ABOVE: *While this knight had died shortly before the siege began, his portrait shows the fine plate armor worn by the men who fought against the Turkish army.*

fenders had died fighting for St. Elmo, but they had taken over 8000 of the enemy, including Dragut, with them. The Turks' supplies were also running low, with dysentry and other diseases ravaging their camp. Morale was further lowered by the ferocity and determination of the defense, and many agreed with Mustapha's comment as he looked out at the fortress at St. Angelo, "If so small a son has cost us so dear, what price shall we have to pay for so large a father?"

After the fall of St. Elmo, the Turks redeployed their forces to begin the attack on the knights' main stronghold. In an attempt to threaten Senglea from the sea, they also dragged 80 ships on rollers over the Mt. Sciberras peninsula into the southern Grand Harbor, which allowed them to bypass Fort St. Angelo. Through July the guns roared and constant attacks were made from both land and sea. Each one was repulsed, but each one caused a few more casualties among the defenders.

Most of the traditional tactics of siege warfare were used, with mining and artillery fire reducing parts of the walls to rubble. Turkish siege towers were also constructed, but the defenders managed to destroy these with cannon fire, and on one occasion even captured one with a sudden counterattack. It was now that de la Valette needed all his powers of inspiration and encouragement, leading his reserves to breaches in the walls and fighting to hold back the frantic assaults.

Both sides were near exhaustion. Turkish casualties were high; supplies had almost run out; the navy were anxious to be home before the autumn storms – and still the defenders showed no signs of breaking. The final blow for the Turks came when a Christian relief force from Sicily landed on the 7 September, comprising some 8000 fresh soldiers, including nearly 300 European knights of the order. Mustapha was forced to give the order to with-

draw, his army being harassed by the relieving troops and de la Valette's cavalry before embarking. Struggling onto their ships, the rearguard of the once mighty army departed the island, leaving behind over 20,000 of their dead. Some 7000 of the defenders had died, including 250-300 knights, and as the last of the Turks disappeared over the horizon, only 600 of de la Valette's men were left on their feet.

The defense of Malta against the Moslem horde quickly became a heroic legend of the Christian world. It also marked the highwater of Ottoman expansion into the Western Mediterranean, and the island remained in the hands of the knights until Napoleon Bonaparte took it almost 230 years later. The lasting monument to the siege, however, is the grand capital city built on Mt. Sciberras soon afterward – the fortress city named after the man who led and inspired his men through five months of fire and fury, the city called Valetta.

LEFT: The Renaissance city of Valetta was built after the siege, on the site of Mount Sciberras. The fortification in the foreground is where Fort St Elmo stood.

Culloden
1746

"We are putting an end to a bad affair."

LORD GEORGE MURRAY

DRUMOSSIE MOOR IS a flat, open tract of land near Culloden House, some four miles to the east of Inverness, on the northeast coast of Scotland. On the morning of 16 April 1746, this bleak heathland was swept by freezing rain and sleet, driven by a penetrating east wind which bit into the two armies forming up opposite each other. The battle they were about to fight would be the last major action on British soil, and would herald the final disintegration of an ancient way of life.

A year earlier, the young Prince Charles Edward Stuart had landed in Scotland in an attempt to regain the British crown abandoned by his grandfather in 1688. Expecting support among the Highland clans and from the French, he hoped to inspire a Jacobite Catholic revolution that would overthrow the Hanoverian and Protestant King George I. His followers scored some dramatic initial successes, sweeping aside the inadequate garrison troops in Scotland and taking the capital city of Edinburgh, before heading south toward London and the Crown. Momentum and excitement took them as far as Derby, before the threat of superior government forces recently brought back from Flanders caused the Jacobites to retreat to Scotland.

They were chased by a large government army under the King's son, William Augustus, Duke of Cumberland, who crossed into Scotland in January 1746. Even though the redcoats suffered a humiliating defeat at Falkirk, by the end of February they had chased the Jacobites north to Inverness, and after pausing in Aberdeen to avoid the worst of the winter snows, Cumberland led his troops northward to continue the pursuit in April. No military genius, he was a competent, methodical commander who had learnt his trade in the hard school of the wars in Europe. Fat and unprepossessing, he was surprisingly popular with his soldiers, and his great achievement was to instill a confi-

LEFT: The Duke of Cumberland accepting the surrender of Carlisle during his northward pursuit of the Highlanders.

RIGHT: Blanchet's portrait of Charles Edward Stuart is a fine image of the "Bonnie Prince Charlie" of song and legend.

PRINCE CHARLES EDWARD
BLANCHET

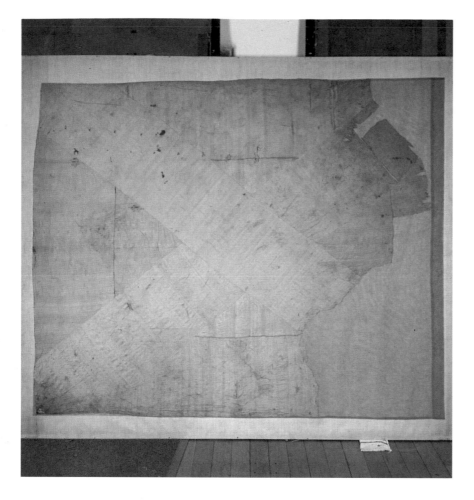

hack the man down with a heavy broadsword, so to counter this, Cumberland's army trained in a new drill, where the soldier would thrust his bayonet into the enemy on his right, to a side where the Highlander would be unprotected. Each redcoat would thus rely on the man to his left to protect him.

Cumberland also had a much more experienced army than that which had been chased out of Scotland the previous year. Long-service veterans of the European wars manned many of his regiments, men who had seen the bloody chaos of battle at Dettingen and Fontenoy. They were formed into battalions, nominally of 815 men but usually nearer 500, each named after their Colonel in Chief. Each man carried a smooth-bore flintlock musket, most using the 46in-long "Brown Bess" Long Land pattern. Able to shoot four or five balls each minute, the musket was a deadly weapon when fired in volleys at ranges of up to 60 yards. For close combat, the musket was fitted with a 17in, triangular-section, socket bayonet.

The army was further strengthened by the addition of a company of the Royal Artillery, with 10 six-pounders on wheeled carriages and a further six high-trajectory mortars. There were also some poorly trained cavalry plus some independent companies and the Argyll Militia – Highland levies from the clans (especially the Campbells) that had sided with the government.

Charles' army was a historical anachronism, largely formed from tribal levies raised by each clan chief. The Highland clans were the last great tribal society in Europe; each group consisting of complex feudal networks of family

ABOVE: This is the actual standard that the Appin Stewarts carried at Culloden.

dence in their own abilities that up till now had been singularly lacking.

The wild screaming charge of the Highlanders in earlier battles had completely unnerved the raw government troops, so Cumberland had spent the winter retraining his army in musket fire, drill and bayonet fighting. The clansmen had used their round shields to sweep aside the long infantry bayonets and

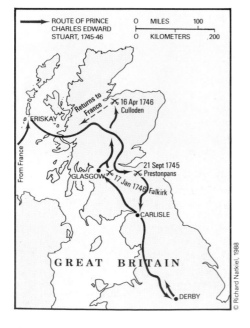

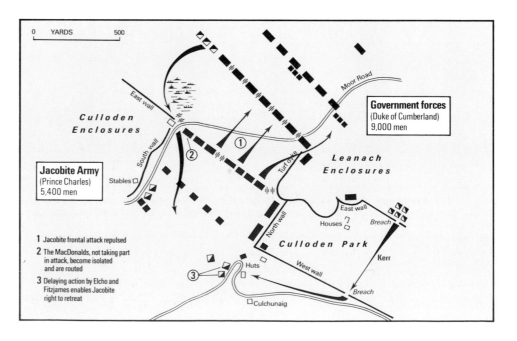

1 Jacobite frontal attack repulsed
2 The MacDonalds, not taking part in attack, become isolated and are routed
3 Delaying action by Elcho and Fitzjames enables Jacobite right to retreat

allegiances. The regiments that stood in the rain at Culloden reflected this, with the chief or his son in the lead, his brothers and younger sons commanding the flanks or rear, and the other officers coming from the heads of the important families of the clan. Each man stood in a position dictated by his social standing, with the poorest sub-tenants in the rear ranks. A number of foreign volunteers also fought with the Jacobite army, including complete regiments of Scots and Irish exiles which were currently in French service – the only practical result of the help promised to Charles by the French king, Louis XV.

The Jacobite generals never had complete control over this quarrelsome mass of proud and independent clans, more used to fighting each other than together as a homogenous army. Charles himself was only 25 years old, a courageous romantic with experience of war but little knowledge of command. His Lieutenant General was Lord George Murray, a 46-year-old veteran who was a skilled and dynamic soldier. Unfortunately for the Jacobite cause, by Culloden he had lost the trust of the Prince, who was more inclined to listen to Quartermaster General John O'Sullivan, an unstable neurotic with little grasp of strategy.

By 15 April 1746, Cumberland's 8000 troops were encamped outside Inverness, within easy reach of the Highlanders on Drumossie moor. That night the Jacobites attempted a surprise night attack on the redcoat camp, but poor planning and organization caused it to be abandoned after a cold, tiring and confusing march across the moors. O'Sullivan's lack of organization also caused the Jacobite food supplies to be left in Inverness, ensuring that the dispirited troops would have to face the coming battle with empty stomachs. Morale was already low after the retreat from Derby, and many of the Highland levies had drifted away, back to their farms and their families.

Charles realized that he could run from the government army no longer, and that a full-scale battle must be fought soon. The moor was not a good place for a Highland army, its firm open ground being ideal for the deployment of the government artillery and cavalry. Murray was aware of this problem and wanted to retreat to another position where boggy ground would neutralize these advantages, but was overruled by the Prince on O'Sullivan's urging. For this battle, the young Stuart would lead his troops himself, ignoring the advice of his most skilled commander.

ABOVE: The colors of Barrell's Regiment, the unit that took the brunt of the Highlanders' charge.

ABOVE LEFT: Lord George Murray was probably the best of the Jacobite generals. Unfortunately his advice to fight elsewhere went unheeded on the morning of the battle.

FAR LEFT: Cumberland's army had chased the Highlanders to Inverness, where they stood and fought at nearby Culloden. The battle map shows the oblique angle of the Jacobite line and the enclosures which fixed their right flank.

FAR RIGHT: An engraving of the battle showing many key events, including the Highland charge to the left of the redcoat line, and the government cavalry outflanking through the enclosures.

BELOW RIGHT: Another contemporary illustration; this one is less accurate.

BELOW: This engraving shows the government army advancing to take possession of the field.

So by midday on the 16th, both armies were lined up facing each other across the rainswept moor. The government's front line was about 700 yards long, and consisted of six regiments of infantry drawn up in three ranks. Behind were a second row of six, then a reserve of two regiments; plus most of the independent companies and the Argyll militia. Cavalry protected both flanks and the guns were deployed in pairs between the frontline regiments. There was no noise or cheering from the government army, and many Highland observers commented on the grim determined silence, the troops marching into position "like a sullen river."

The Highland line was in some disarray. Only 5000 men stood there, with nearly 2000 missing, either as stragglers, deserters or foragers for food. The front line was where most of the clan regiments stood, but due to lack of firm central control the line ran at an oblique angle to that of the enemy. Murray commanded the right wing and his Atholl brigade, which lined up opposite Barrell's regiment on Cumberland's left. Lord John Drummond commanded the center, and the Duke of Perth the left, where the various MacDonald contingents stood grumbling about their displacement from their traditional position on the right of the line. The second and third line was comprised of lowland volunteers and the remnants of Jacobite cavalry squadrons, many of dubious effectiveness. Here also were the French Royal Scots, and the Franco-Irish Fitzjames Horse and Irish Piquets.

The Jacobite right was only 400-500 yards from the enemy, while the MacDonalds on the extreme left were at least 700 yards distant, which meant that the line would not be able to charge the redcoats as a compact mass. Murray tried to have this deployment corrected, but the young Prince seemed unwilling or unable to control his quarrelsome subordinates, and let it stand. Murray was also worried about his right flank, where a series of high stone walls fenced off the farming enclosures of Leanach, Culwhiniac and Culchunaig, fearing that an enemy force could get behind these to attack the Jacobite rear. He was told not to worry about this by O'Sullivan.

The first shot was fired at around 1300 hours from a Jacobite cannon, the ball flying over the government front ranks in an attempt to hit the Duke and his staff. After a few more of these largely ineffectual shots, the order was given for the government artillery to open fire. Thick grey smoke rolled toward the Jacobites as the cannonballs plunged into the ranks of standing men, tearing great gaps in their lines. The inexperienced Jacobite gunners soon abandoned their weapons, leaving the government army to stand virtually unscathed. Cumberland was content to let his guns carry out this slaughter, but he knew the enemy could not withstand it for long and that the wild charge must come soon. He brought Pultney's Regiment from his third line to the front, moved some of his cavalry forward, and ordered Wolfe's Regiment forward of his front line, to the left flank.

Protected by the walls of Leanach farm, they faced along the government line, able to fire into the flank of any attackers.

In the Jacobite lines, chaos ensued as men choked in the gunsmoke while others were knocked to the ground, their limbs smashed or torn away by the steady fire. Clansmen pleaded for the order to charge, but the Prince, who had moved farther to the rear to escape the gunfire, was caught in a morass of indecision. Eventually after over 20 minutes of slaughter and after some of his finest regiments had lost over one third of their men, he gave the order to attack. By then it was too late – command and control within the Jacobite army had already collapsed.

Without waiting for the order, Clan Chattan surged forward into the grapeshot and smoke, yelling their anger and frustration and desperate to get to grips with their tormentors. A confederation of Mackintoshes, MacGillivrays and MacBeans, they were closely followed by the Camerons, the Appin Stewarts, then the whole of the Jacobite right wing. In the confusion, Chattan swerved to the right, colliding with their neighbors and pressing the Athollmen on the far right against the walls of Culwhiniac and Leanach. While the Highlanders milled about in the smoke, the massed ranks of Cumberland's infantry finally opened fire, the long ragged volleys adding to the confusion.

THE COUNT OF ALBANY.
PRINCE CHARLES EDWARD STUART.

The Highlanders were funneled farther to the right, only to be savaged from their flank by the steady fire of Wolfe's Regiment. Nevertheless, their charge had such momentum that nearly 1500 men came screaming out of the smoke, slamming into Barrell's and Munro's on the extreme left of the government line. Barrell's took the full force of the assault, but unfortunately for the Jacobites they were experienced veterans who had already proven their mettle at Falkirk. Savage hand-to-hand fighting broke out, with some platoons falling back in good order on Sempill's Regiment in the second line. Some of the Highlanders managed to penetrate the front line, but most made no headway against the resolute government troopers. Within a few minutes the attack had lost its momentum, and with shot still pouring in from Wolfe's Regiment on their right, many of the Highlanders started to stream back in panic toward their own lines.

On the left of the Jacobite line, The Duke of Perth had great difficulty in persuading the sullen MacDonalds to attack. Eventually they charged forward over the sodden ground, running over 700 yards through grape shot and musket fire. They never reached the government line, although they repeatedly charged to within a few yards then retreated, hoping to entice the redcoats to break ranks and come forward. Cumberland's cavalry eventually moved around their flank, attacking the remnants of the MacDonalds as they retired in disarray, leaving behind the body of their Chieftain.

Meanwhile on Cumberland's left, a mixed force of Hawley's dragoons and Argyll Militia breached the stone walls of the enclosures and moved around the collapsing right flank of the Highlanders, with the Campbells settling some old scores by attacking the Camerons as they pulled back. A tiny contingent of 60 Irishmen from Fitzjames' Horse managed to hold back this force of over 500 dragoons, allowing many Highlanders time to escape. The Irish Picquets and the French Royal Scots Regiment also held out grimly against the cavalry on the Jacobite left, providing a last service to the now collapsing army. As the Highlander's defeat became evident, their "Bonnie Prince" rode away, leaving his followers to their fate.

The Jacobite revolution was finished in one bloody spasm lasting less than an hour. The Highlanders that remained in intact military formation marched off to the south, leaving more than 1500 of their number lying dead and dying on the moor. Cumberland's troops made the required token advance on to the battleground, having lost only about 60 men with 260 wounded. Once the fighting was over, it was the turn of the cavalry to earn their glory, and this

PREVIOUS PAGES: When Morier created his famous painting of the battle he used actual Highlander prisoners as models.

FAR LEFT: Charles Edward Stuart ended his days in Italy, as a sad, lonely man living on brandy and memories.

BELOW: While this Victorian illustration is somewhat melodramatic, it illustrates the savage repression of the Highlands undertaken after the rebellion was crushed.

LEFT: The bleak Drumossie Moor as it is today, with memorial stones marking the initial positions of the clan regiments. In the opening phase of the battle, the Duke of Cumberland's artillery, firing into the ranks of the clans across this featureless moorland, caused great casualties thereby goading a number of the Highland army's units into charging the government lines. Only on the government's left did the charge strike home, elsewhere along the line controlled volley fire and grapeshot devastated the clansmen before they could get to grips with the English. The defeat of the Highlanders who had reached the government line ended the battle; the uprising had been thwarted in less than one hour.

they did with the gusto of men safe from danger, riding the road to Inverness, hacking down fleeing enemy and any unfortunate civilians that got in their way. On the battlefield, the wounded were dispatched by the soldiers, some of the bodies also being preyed upon by the usual collection of thieves, beggars and scavengers that follow a battle. No quarter was given to most of the rebels, although surrender terms were given to the "regular" troops of the French-Scots and Irish contingents.

The end of the 1745 rebellion was to see some of the most savage repression carried out by a British government on its own citizens, with hangings, executions and jailings rife in an attempt to pacify the Highland regions. Legislation designed to destroy, once and for all, this wild, archaic way of life was also enacted, with prohibitions on traditional dress and weapons. This was to be the first stage in the destruction of a people. The sundering of the historic bonds of clan and kinship begun after Culloden would see their final conclusion in the empty glens, burnt cottages and packed immigrant ships of the nineteenth century.

Quebec
1759

"I shall be induced, in support of an ill-gotten reputation, to be lavish of my life, and shall probably meet that fate which is the ordinary effect of such conduct."

MAJOR GENERAL JAMES WOLFE

FAR RIGHT: *A thin, sickly man, Wolfe nevertheless possessed great courage and was popular with his men.*

BELOW: *A schematic view of Quebec city, showing both the main upper level and the buildings along the waterfront.*

IN 1759, A recently revitalized British administration launched an expedition designed to eradicate the French colonies in North America. Britain and France had long been at war, and the conflict had spilled over into the young continent as both sides and their colonists struggled for supremacy, with the native population caught in the middle. This new British effort would see the dispatch of a force that was larger and better-equipped than those previously sent, which would combine with the forces already in place in a multi-pronged offensive on the French colony. The most important attack would be on the capital, Quebec, which could be reached by sailing an expedition inland up the St Lawrence river.

To carry out this plan, 8500 soldiers and some 200 warships and transports were dispatched under the overall command of the young Colonel James Wolfe. Promoted to local Major General for this expedition, Wolfe was a sickly, frail figure, who despite constant illness,

I.S.C.Schaak Pinx.t   Rich.d Houston Fecit

Major Gen.l James Wolfe,
COMMANDER in Chief of his Majesty's FORCES
on the Expedition against Quebec.

had by 1759 managed to pack a great deal of military experience into his 32 years. He had fought at Dettingen and Culloden, had taken part in the suppression of the Scottish Highlands, and had already experienced the difficulties of war in the Americas. He was a thoughtful soldier who took great care over the details of his profession, possessing a keen intellect and being unafraid to react quickly to unexpected opportunities. Wolfe also had a reputation for leading from the front and exposing himself to the same risks as his men, a tendency guaranteed to win the respect and affection of the common soldier. The force he was given was also exceptional, with a core of 10 experienced battalions of hard-bitten British regulars, veterans of fighting in Europe and North America. Other elements of his force included a composite unit formed from the grenadier companies of three other regiments, six companies of American Rangers (frontiersmen enlisted for full-time service) and three batteries of artillery.

The French defenders were nominally under the command of Louis-Joseph, the Marquis de Montcalm, although constant friction between him and the civilian Governor-

ABOVE: *The Marquis de Montcalm was an experienced and capable soldier, although at Quebec he was outmaneuvered by Wolfe.*

RIGHT: *A British soldier from his battalion's grenadier company. While trained to use grenades, these men were also regarded as elite shock troops.*

FAR RIGHT: *A private soldier of the 48th Foot, this man has the lapels of his coat buttoned back. He also wears red breeches and the brown gaiters commonly worn on campaign.*

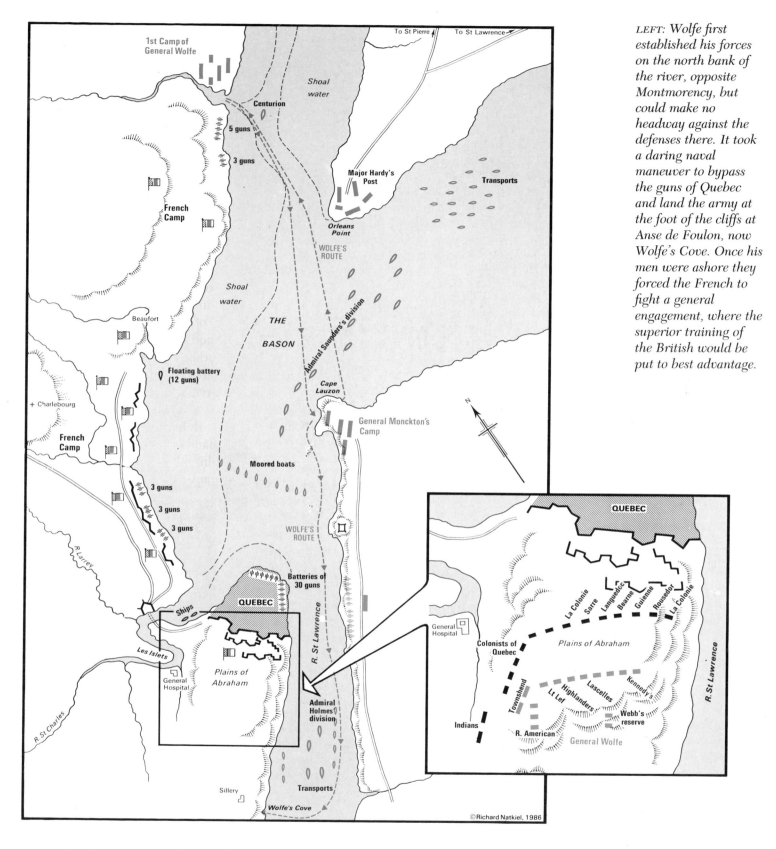

© Richard Natkiel, 1986

LEFT: Wolfe first established his forces on the north bank of the river, opposite Montmorency, but could make no headway against the defenses there. It took a daring naval maneuver to bypass the guns of Quebec and land the army at the foot of the cliffs at Anse de Foulon, now Wolfe's Cove. Once his men were ashore they forced the French to fight a general engagement, where the superior training of the British would be put to best advantage.

General, the Marquis de Vaudreuil would prove a fatal hindrance in the battle to come. Montcalm's army of 14,000 was larger than Wolfe's, but was largely composed of local militia and the civilian city garrison, supplemented by about 1000 Native Americans and a small professional force of five understrength French regular battalions. His only real hope was to sit behind his fortifications and try and hold the British until the winter, in the hope of receiving reinforcements from France in the new year.

Quebec sat on a small promontory on the north bank of the St. Lawrence, with the much smaller St. Charles river running along the northwest side. In 1759 the city was protected to the north and south by a rocky shore and

high cliffs, with stone-built fortifications on the western, landward side. These defenses were not particularly well designed and could be overlooked and enfiladed from high ground outside the city. On the southeast side of the city itself was a low waterfront town and harbor, although there was a steep cliff a few yards inland, above which sat the main part of the city.

The only place where a landing could be easily made was on the banks of the St. Lawrence to the east of the city, so defensive fortifications had been built here for about four miles until they met the Montmorency river, whose steep and wooded banks provided good flanking protection inland. Other defensive preparations included floating gun batteries placed in the St. Lawrence and St. Charles, although the French neglected to place any fortifications either on the south banks of the St Lawrence or on Orleans, a large island a mile or so downstream. Their real hope was that the river itself would prove too difficult for a large fleet to find passage and that a major attack on Quebec would never materialize – an attitude that would cost them dearly.

They had reckoned without the sailing skills of the Royal Navy, and by mid-June Wolfe's army had established a base camp on Orleans while landing the bulk of their force at Montmorency, just outside the eastern edge of the French fortifications. An artillery battery was emplaced at Point Levis, a high promontory on the south bank of the river, directly opposite the city. Within a few days the guns started a constant bombardment which continued for the rest of the siege. They caused immense damage, wrecking hundreds of buildings and causing many severe fires.

A number of skirmishes took place in July while Wolfe decided upon his plan of action. The first real attack was on 31 July, when two shallow-bottomed boats loaded with grenadiers were deliberately run aground just west of Montmorency. The idea was a limited assault to capture a French redoubt, but the assault failed. A combination of a previously undiscovered sandbank which prevented the fire support warships from getting close enough to the shore, stronger defenses than expected, and a hasty, uncoordinated attack all contributed to the repulse.

ABOVE: Wolfe launched his first attack against the defenses at Beauport, landing men from the river. They were easily repulsed by heavy musket fire.

FAR LEFT: This French corporal is typical of the regular troops under Montcalm's command. Their efficiency was hampered by the incorporation of militia companies into their lines.

ABOVE: Vice-Admiral
Charles Saunders was
a skilled officer who
commanded Wolfe's
naval forces.

RIGHT: This Captain is
in the Languedoc
Regiment, one of the
regular French
battalions present at
Quebec.

ABOVE: A more accurate view of Quebec, drawn by Wolfe's aide-de-camp, Captain Hervey Smyth.

Throughout August, Wolfe's forces continued to besiege the city, while carrying out a campaign of terror and destruction in the Canadian settlements downriver. The navy had already sailed small numbers of ships upstream which had passed relatively unscathed under the guns of Quebec, so Wolfe sent a brigade under James Murray upstream to harass the French lines of communications by landing at various points to attack supply dumps and settlements. This posed such a threat to Montcalm's supplies that he had to send 1000 men under Bougainville to shadow Murray, and the two sides played a cat-and-mouse game up and down the river for the next month.

Wolfe seems to have spent this time almost paralysed by uncharacteristic indecision, considering one plan after another but deciding on none. His sickness was sapping his energy and the sure touch of the skilled commander seems to have left him during this period. The plan finally decided upon was actually put forward by his brigadiers, after they had discounted various ideas proposed by their commander. The army would withdraw to the south bank of the river, march upstream, then be carried across the river in the fleet of transports to land above Quebec. They would have to overcome

the steep cliffs on the north bank, although reconnaissance had shown that there may be one or two places where troops could land. Daring and dangerous, should the plan succeed the British army would be positioned on the heights above the city, astride Montcalm's line of communications. They already knew from deserters that there was virtually no food in the city, so Montcalm would have to come out and face them in open battle, a type of action ideally suited to the training and experience of Wolfe's redcoats.

The end of August saw a sudden burst of action, and by the first week in September the army had pulled back and concentrated upstream of Quebec, with many of the troops already embarked aboard ship, ready to be landed. Montcalm seems not to have realized the danger, expecting Wolfe to double back and make an assault either on the city itself or against his landward defenses.

On the night of 12 September 1759, a flotilla of flat-bottomed boats packed with British soldiers slid silently along the St. Lawrence river, their oars gently pulling against the strong current. These troops, led by a hand-picked detachment of light infantry, were the first wave and were expected to storm the

French piquets overlooking the chosen landing site at Anse de Foulon. Legend has it that they were challenged by a sentry who was satisfied by the vague answer given by a French-speaking officer in one of the boats, but whatever the truth, they were not identified as enemy until the first landings had taken place.

The current had swept the British past their planned landing site and they found themselves landing below a steep shale slope, dotted with scrub and trees. The soldiers in their heavy fighting order had to scramble up this hill, pulling themselves upward by clinging on to the sparse vegetation. Eventually they reached the top, and after exchanging a few shots with the French sentries, secured the narrow track that was their first objective. Wolfe was in this first wave, and quickly took command of the tiny beachhead, urging the rest of his men upward as their boats crunched ashore. The second wave now came in, landing from larger transport vessels and being ferried across from the south bank.

By daybreak, over 4500 men and two cannon had been successfully put ashore and were arraying in battle order on the heights (sometimes known as the Plains of Abraham) above

the landward defenses of the city. A night amphibious landing on an unknown hostile shore is one of the most difficult and dangerous military tasks, and this one was a superb combination of planning and improvisation, all without the modern benefits of powered boats, helicopters and radio communications.

Response from the French was sluggish, and it took them some hours to realize the full extent of the disaster. The reports that Montcalm initially received indicated that the landing was a feint, an analysis which fitted in with his expectations. As he rode from his camp in Montmorency to see for himself, he was shocked to see the bright red coats of Wolfe's army standing in fighting array, their fixed bayonets like a forest of thorns. He immediately realized that he could not withstand a siege, and that his only hope was to attack and try and drive the British away from his lines of supply. His next orders were to become a matter of controversy, as rather than wait for Bougainville's detachment to return from upriver, he decided to make a hasty attack straight away, with the forces immediately to hand.

The British battalions were drawn up across the plain in two ranks rather than the custom-

BELOW: A model of one of the barges used to land Wolfe's assault troops. Each boat carried about 50 soldiers as well as its crew of 21.

ABOVE: A copy of West's painting of the death of Wolfe. The artist concentrated more on the drama than historical accuracy.

TOP: A 1759 view of the fall of Quebec, showing many of the major events: the soldiers landing by boat, the scramble up the cliffs, the tussle for possession of the only path, the naval guns coming ashore, and the final battle on the plains above.

ary three, in an effort to extend the line. As they stood waiting for the French to march out toward them, the redcoats came under harassing fire from the flanks, as Canadian militia and colonial regulars tangled with the British riflemen and light infantry skirmishers in the woods and outskirts of the city. The cannons were also firing by now and causing casualties to both sides, although grapeshot from the two British guns (manned by Royal Navy seamen) was especially effective.

The French formed up three groups, their total strength being about the same as the 4500 British. However, there was a great disparity in the quality and experience of the troops. The redcoats were almost all hardened veterans, about to fight in the way they knew best, while the French were very much a mixed force of amateurs leavened by a small force of regulars. When the order was given to advance, the French army poured forward, with Montcalm at their head on a black horse. Things went wrong from the start as the colonial irregulars were not trained to move in the tight disciplined formations necessary for such a battle. "We had not gone twenty paces," wrote one officer, "when the left was too far in rear and the center too far in front." When they were about 120 yards from the British, the French fired a ragged volley, too far away to be really effective. Some then dropped to the ground to reload their muskets, while others came on, the whole attack degenerating into a chaotic shambles. Still the British stood awaiting the order to open fire.

When the French came within 60 yards, some British units opened fire by platoons, but it was not until the enemy were as close as 40 yards that the order for a general volley was given. The "Brown Bess" muskets roared out along the line in one long rolling blast, the balls smashing into the disorganized formations. Within a few minutes, the devastating, disciplined fire ripped apart the French, and their cohesion collapsed completely, with men streaming back toward the city. The British advanced in pursuit, although they were hindered by fire from Canadian irregulars on the flanks, some of whom made a gallant stand in a wooded hill to the north of the battlefield. By the end of the day, the British had suffered only 58 dead and 600 wounded, while the French had at least 600 dead.

The lasting irony of this battle and the stuff of legend was the fate of the two rival commanders. As the French began shooting, Wolfe was hit on the wrist, but after having his hand roughly bandaged stayed in the front line. A few minutes later he was hit in the chest, and possibly in the groin at the same time. These wounds were fatal, and he died within minutes, supposedly just after being informed of the French rout. At almost the same time, Montcalm was hit in the stomach and thigh, possibly by artillery fragments. He rode back to Quebec but was to die the next day.

This short, sharp confrontation was the beginning of the end of French control in Canada. Quebec surrendered almost instantly, while the remnants of the French army escaped inland to find shelter for the winter. Under British control, Quebec withstood a second siege by the French in the following year, but this time it stood, and by the end of that summer, the last French armies in Canada had surrendered.

BELOW: A remarkably similar rendition of the death of Montcalm, with natives and vegetation transported from tropical Africa.

The Alamo
1836

"The victory will cost the enemy so dear, that it will be worse for him than a defeat."

LT. COL. WILLIAM B. TRAVIS

BELOW: Antonio Lopez de Santa Anna was a corrupt, ruthless and devious politician, nicknamed Don Demonio (Sir Devil) *by his countrymen.*

THE MEXICAN PROVINCE of Tejas (or Texas) was proving difficult to populate with Spanish and Mexican colonists, so in the early nineteenth century the government encouraged thousands of Americans to settle, enticing them with promises of land. After Mexico gained independence from Spain in 1831, it quickly came under the control of Antonio Lopez de Santa Anna, a ruthless and corrupt politician and soldier, who by a mixture of intrigue and force had taken over the government and effectively destroyed the liberal constitution of 1824. Many American settlers in Texas (who referred to themselves as Texians), were wary of Santa Anna's rule, and wanted Texas to be either an independent state, or part of the United States of America; while others simply opposed the oppressive measures of the new regime, being loyal to the original 1824 constitution. Conflict with Santa Anna was inevitable, and when a punitive expedition under General Martin Perfecto de Cos established itself at San Antonio de Bexar, violence soon erupted.

In preparation for a fight, the settlers had formed a citizen's army which also received volunteers and support from many Americans. A colorful group of self-reliant individuals who lacked almost all forms of military discipline and control, they took most of their decisions by democratic vote. Their strength was that of men fighting for their freedom, although many were also ex-soldiers with military skills, and others who lived in the wilds were superb marksmen. Their first action was an attack on Cos, and after four days of bitter close-quarters fighting the 300 Texians ejected the 1400 Mexicans from San Antonio and the fortified mission known as the Alamo.

Many believed that the war was won, and drifted back to their homes, farms and businesses. Some were so carried away by the victory that they launched an ill-prepared sortie into Mexican territory, which soon ended in disaster. The newly-formed Texian government, however, was under no illusions, and knew that the Mexicans would return in overwhelming force. The Texians were still gathering their strength under Sam Houston and could not face this army in open combat. Their only chance was to withdraw into the country, harassing and delaying the Mexicans as they advanced, in the hope that they would be sufficiently weakened over time to allow for an effective counterattack once the Texian army was fully formed. San Antonio and the Alamo could not be held, so Houston ordered James Bowie, a renowned businessman and duellist (of "Bowie" knife fame) who held a reserve Colonel's commission, to organize the evacuation of the tiny garrison and the dismantling of their defenses.

When Bowie arrived, he found the garrison of about 80 men under Colonel James Neill in a sorry state, their clothes ragged and their food stocks almost finished. In a surprising decision which moved Houston to fury, he chose to ignore his orders and decided to fortify the mission and stand firm. Bowie realized that Santa Anna would have to invade Texas using the old Spanish road through San Antonio, and that time and resources spent attacking the Alamo would give Houston more time to gather his strength. Houston almost resigned over this

LEFT: James Bowie was sent to destroy the Alamo Mission and withdraw the troops. Instead, he decided to stand and fight.

BELOW: An overall view of the mission, it shows the roofless chapel, the cattle pen and the main compound with the water ditch along its length. The building along the near wall of the compound was actually longer than shown, while that on the far side was shorter.

West front of Church.

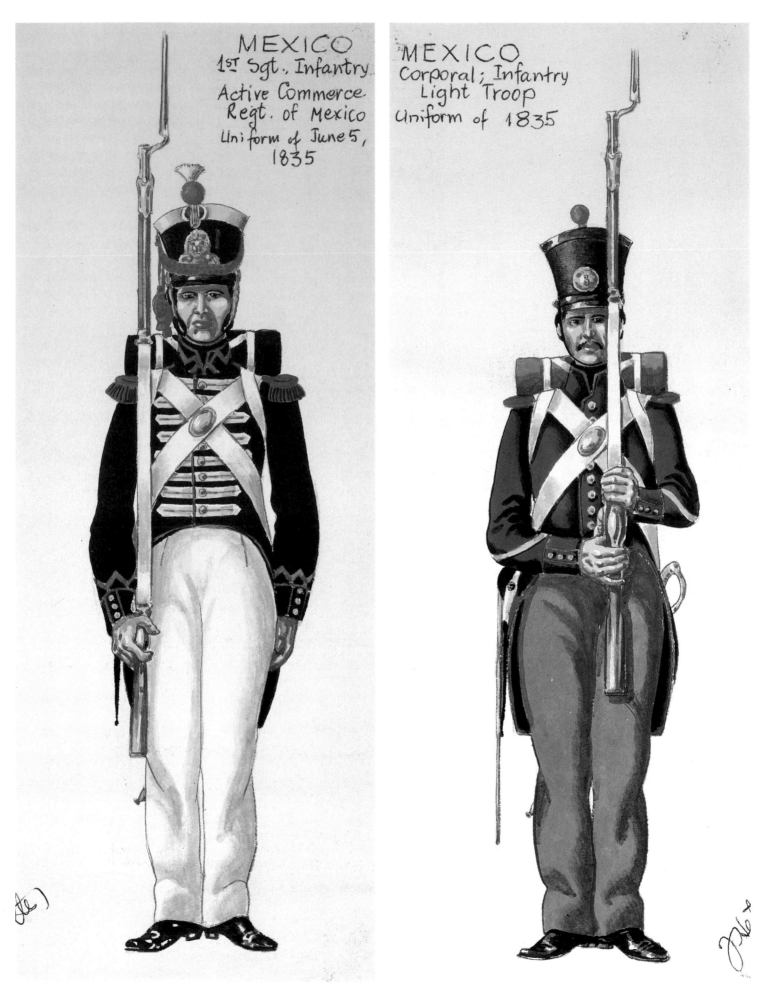

MEXICO
1ST Sgt., Infantry
Active Commerce
Regt. of Mexico
Uniform of June 5,
1835

MEXICO
Corporal; Infantry
Light Troop
Uniform of 1835

disobedience, but Governor Smith managed to persuade him not to, and also arranged for some reinforcements to be sent.

William B. Travis led a detachment of 30 men which arrived at the Alamo on 3 February, five days before a company of Tennessee volunteers under Colonel David Crockett rode in. Travis, a South Carolinan lawyer with a regular commission as a Lieutenant Colonel, was a flamboyant character who was fond of theatrical statements and posturing, but he had a firm sense of destiny and purpose. Crockett was also larger than life. Starting out as a hunter and an Indian fighter, he had become a US Congressman and a national hero. His attitude was typified by his statement "All the honor I desire is that of defending the liberties of our common country."

Friction arose when Neill went on leave, perhaps intimidated by the powerful leaders who had arrived to help him. As Bowie only held a reserve commission, Travis was left in command as the senior regular officer. The older and more experienced Bowie was disgusted by this, returning to the whiskey bottle which had already wrecked his health since the death of his wife and children three years previously. Nevertheless, he commanded respect from many of the volunteers, so as a compromise Travis offered to share command.

Efforts were being made to improve the defenses and lay in supplies, when on 23 February 1836, Santa Anna's army of over 2000 soldiers marched into San Antonio, over a month earlier than anticipated. Travis hurriedly gathered his men into the fortified mis-

FAR LEFT: The Mexican infantry based their uniforms and equipment on European patterns. The man on the far left is a corporal in a light infantry unit while the figure on his right is a sergeant in a militia battalion.

BELOW: William B. Travis was a flamboyant figure, a lawyer and patriot given to dramatic gestures.

FAR RIGHT: The legendary scene when Travis asked for volunteers to stay, and to indicate their decision by crossing a line drawn on the ground. Every man but one crossed the line, with James Bowie even being carried over on his sickbed.

sion, a tiny force of some 150 with around 25 non-combatants and family members. Santa Anna initially offered surrender terms to the Texians, but when this was refused he raised a red flag over the church at San Fernando, the sinister signal that no quarter would be given.

The defenses were centered around the mission church, a strong-walled building even if it had no roof at the time. Adjoining this were a convent yard and cattle pen, again protected by earthen walls and a pallisade fence. To the west was a large open compound surrounded by an earthen wall, with a narrow water ditch running along its length. The east side of this square was bound by a long, narrow building, the "long barracks," the most central part of the whole mission and where Travis planned to make his final stand. The settlers were far too few to man the whole perimeter effectively, but their saving grace was an ample supply of artillery. Some 20 guns of various types were mounted on earthen platforms around the walls and were able to give devastating fire in all directions. Sources differ on the exact position and composition of the guns, but most agree that they included a number of 8-pounders, a massive 18-pounder and a naval carronade.

Santa Anna immediately gave the order to emplace his siege batteries, and by 24 February they started a steady bombardment. The same day saw Bowie's health finally give out, and he retired to his sickbed with Travis taking sole command. Mexican artillery pounded at the defenses, damaging great areas of wall and knocking down parts of most buildings. The Mexicans also attempted to cow the Texians with sniping fire, but long rifles in the hands of Crockett's frontiersmen easily outranged and outshot their smooth-bore muskets. Texian guns returned the fire, although most of the Mexicans were kept out of range.

Santa Anna's soldiers had encircled the mission, although his cavalry patrols and outposts never managed to completely seal the defenders off from the outside world. All through the siege Travis was able to send couriers with messages, whether dramatic and heroic statements of intent or desperate requests for help from the towns of Gonzales and Goliad. The only reinforcements that arrived were 32 volunteers under Captain Kimball who rode through the Mexican lines on 1 March, providing a much-needed boost to morale.

As the siege continued, Santa Anna realized that the defenses were weakest to the north, so by the end of February he had another battery

FAR RIGHT: Probably the most accurate painting of the final assault on the mission, although the actual attack took place at dawn. The Mexicans can be seen streaming into the compound and firing a captured cannon at the long barracks. Another column assaults the low palisade, while the last defenders cluster inside the chapel.

emplaced here. Inside the mission, powder and shot were running low, causing fire to be slackened to conserve ammunition for the assault which must come soon. Travis realized that they could not hold out much longer, and in an assembly on 5 March he gave his men a last chance to escape before the inevitable end. Legend has it that he drew a line in the sand, saying that all those who intended to stay should cross the line, and the same legend has Bowie being carried across the line in his sickbed. Whatever was actually said and done, all but one of his 183 men elected to stay at a time when escape was still possible – a decision that resonates through American and Texan history to this day.

That evening saw the guns tear a wide breach in the north wall of the courtyard, while the defenders desperately tried to fill it with a hastily-built stockade. The firing stopped that night, and both attacker and defender waited patiently for the final assault the next morning. Just before dawn, the Mexican army advanced, split into four separate columns. Three companies of infantry attacked from the south, two from the east, while the main attack was to be from the north. This was itself divided into two columns, with Colonel Duca leading nearly two battalions from the northeast and Cos leading a similar sized force from the northwest. In all, 1800 men surged forward, advancing in open formation with fixed bayonets, while some carried scaling ladders and crowbars to overcome the defensive fortifications.

Most of the Texians manning the walls had prepared three or four loaded weapons, and managed to put up a withering fire while their cannon blasted grapeshot into the advancing men. The columns coming from the northeast and east were devastated by the gunfire, never even reaching the walls of the courtyard, but the other two pressed forward against the ramparts. A savage close-quarters struggle ensued, during which Travis was killed by a musket ball to the head. This attack was eventually repulsed, with the Mexicans pulling back to regroup for another attempt. The second assault was consolidated into two columns, one each from the north and south respectively. After this too was thrown back, Santa Anna's reserve companies were added to the third attack, which finally crashed through the stockade protecting the breach in the northwest wall. At the same time, the southern assault captured the 18-pounder cannon at the southwest corner of the courtyard, and men began to pour over the

wall. Most of the surviving Texians fell back from the walls into the long barracks, but Crockett and his men were caught in the open and hacked down.

As the defenders regrouped in the long barracks, they still poured continuous fire into the compound, forcing the attackers to take cover in the shallow water trench. The Mexicans responded by turning around the newly-captured

ABOVE: *A more imaginative view of the final assault, showing the chapel with its later "humped" roof.*

ABOVE RIGHT: *Colonel David Crockett, the renowned frontiersman, Indian fighter and congressman.*

RIGHT: *Another dramatic but inaccurate view, this time with Santa Anna shown in the thick of the fighting.*

FAR RIGHT: *The Mexicans allowed Susannah Dickinson, her daughter and Travis' negro slave to leave unmolested.*

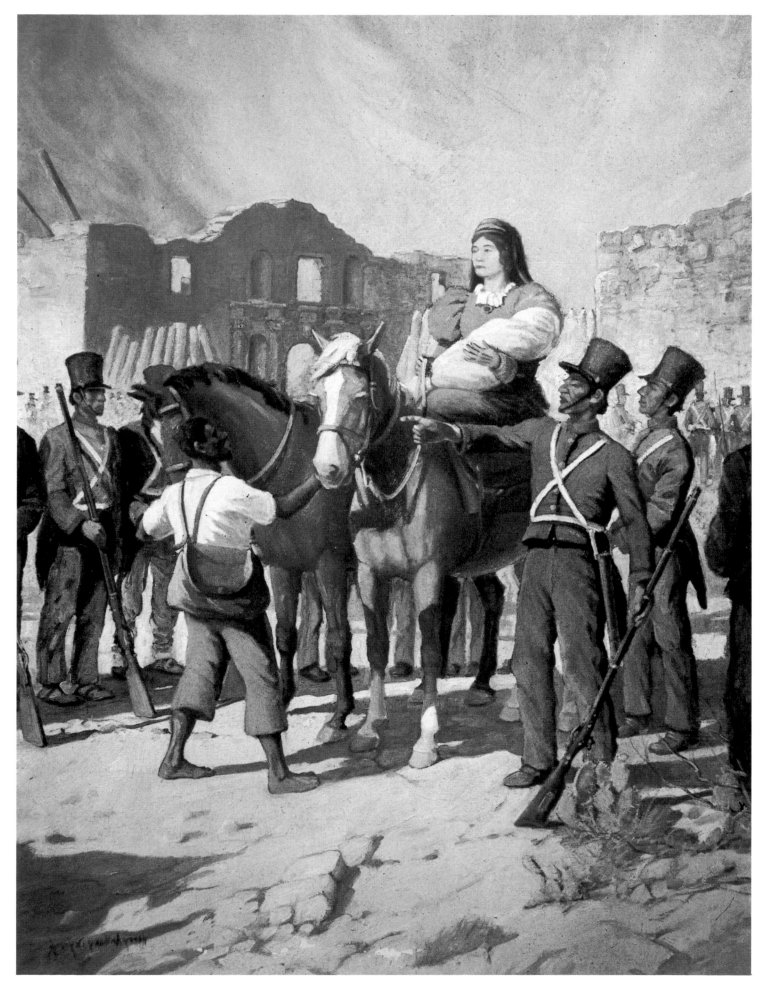

cannon and using them to blast gaping holes in the low building. Within a few minutes they launched a final rush which overwhelmed the defenders, most of whom were bayoneted within the wreckage of the barracks. The last defenders were a small group in the church, but point-blank fire from the captured 18-pounder blew open the door before they were overwhelmed by one final charge.

It had taken less than an hour and a half to secure the Alamo, during which time all but one of the 183 defenders were killed, some after being taken prisoner. Around 200 Mexicans lay dead, with another 400 or so seriously wounded and unable to take any further part in the war. Surprisingly, after such a bitter struggle, the non-combatants were treated with sympathy and the women and children, together with Travis' negro servant, were

allowed to leave the Alamo unharmed. Santa Anna had achieved his victory but the high price paid for it was to influence the conduct of the rest of the war.

Like many other heroic stands, the legend of the men who chose to die rather than surrender their freedom galvanized those who had until then been relatively unmoved by the struggle. Money, volunteers and supplies poured in from America, enabling Houston to create and train an effective army of over 800. In a surprise attack near the River San Jacinto, his men swept aside the Mexicans, destroying their army, and finally winning the independence for Texas which paved the way for eventual incorporation into the Union. As Houston's men stormed through the Mexican camp, their battle cry was one that has become an American icon – "Remember the Alamo!"

FAR LEFT: *Most of the cannon captured by the Mexicans were wrecked then buried before they left. These barrels have been dug up again much later.*

BELOW: *The earliest known photograph of the Alamo, taken around 1852. The picture shows the chapel with a new roof and humped facade, both added after the battle, in 1850.*

Vicksburg

1863

"The problem for us was to move forward to a decisive victory, or our cause was lost. No progress was being made in any other field, and we had to go on."

ULYSSES S. GRANT

FAR RIGHT: An untidy appearance and a relaxed manner belied the clever strategic brain and iron determination of General Grant.

BELOW: The city of Vicksburg controlled transit north and south along the Mississippi River.

WHEN IN THE late summer of 1862, Brigadier General Ulysses S. Grant launched his Union Army of Tennessee toward Vicksburg, the Civil War had been raging for well over a year. The armies in the east had fought each other to a bloody stalemate in and around the hundred miles or so between Washington and Richmond, and it was only in the west that the Union had made significant advances. Kentucky and half of Tennessee were now under Union control, as was part of northern Mississippi, while New Orleans and Baton Rouge

had been taken by Admiral Farragut in a naval assault from the south. The mighty Mississippi river which flowed from north to south and cut the Confederacy in two was close to being wholly in northern hands.

The key to the river was the fortress town of Vicksburg, nearly 200 miles upstream from New Orleans. Built on steep bluffs overlooking a sharp bend in the river, the town was protected on the landward sides by the most extensive earthworks and entrenchments seen to date in the war. Held by the Confederate Army

RIGHT: *William T. Sherman was Grant's protege, and quickly grasped his ideas of making war against the economy of the enemy.*

of Mississippi under John C. Pemberton, its guns prevented the Union from using the river as a supply and communications artery between its northern and southern forces, while ensuring the ability of the Confederates to transport men and material along the 200 miles of river still under their control.

The capture of this fortress was an essential element of the Union's strategy in the west, and Grant intended to attack during the winter, sending his army in a two-pronged approach from Memphis. Sherman, with two corps, was to sail 250 miles downriver, transported by the steamboats of Admiral Porter, to assault the town from the river. Grant would march another column overland to make a simultaneous attack from the eastern, landward side. The plan came unstuck almost immediately after Sherman set out, when Confederate cavalry destroyed most of Grant's supply dumps at Holly Springs, while another raid ripped up miles of railroad behind his army. Without rail supply, Grant could no longer countenance taking such a large force overland in winter, and was forced to cancel his part in the plan. Unfortunately, Sherman was unaware of the disaster, and by the end of December he had landed his 32,000 men in the swamps and bayous of the River Yazoo to the northeast of Vicksburg. On the 29th he launched an assault on the well-defended high ground of Chicksaw bluffs, expecting Grant's men to have been pressing the Confederates from the east. The defenders easily repulsed this attack, inflicting nearly 1800 casualties in exchange for some 200. Sherman withdrew to the northwest, planning to winter on the banks of the Mississippi some 12 miles away.

Grant sailed down the river to join Sherman, and the army spent the rest of the winter in the swamps, shivering under the constant rain and suffering many casualties due to disease and fatigue. It was obvious that Vicksburg could not be taken from the river, and that Grant had to get his army across the river and on to the firm ground to the east of the town. The best place to cross was farther south of the town, but this meant that Porter's transports would have to sail past the guns of the fortress. The river made a sharp bend toward Vicksburg, so Grant's engineers tried to cut a canal across this bend, thus allowing the boats to sail past, out of range of the guns. However, problems with the water level and difficulties in digging and construction prevented this becoming a reality. Another attempt to cut a much longer route

through the Louisiana swamps from higher up the river also failed due to the difficulties with the terrain. Porter then attempted to sail down the Yazoo river from the north, which would have given a decent landing site to the northeast of the city, but this was halted by thick swamps and Confederate defenses. A fourth attempt tried to sail around the thick swamps just above Vicksburg, but was again thwarted by a combination of terrain and enemy action.

Typhoid and dysentry were sweeping through his swamp-bound troops, but as the weather improved Grant remained totally determined to find a way through. As the swamps dried, he decided to risk sending the bulk of his army down the west bank of the river to a point below Vicksburg. He still needed his boats to ferry the troops across the river, so he resolved to sail them downstream, under the guns of Vicksburg. Some ironclad gunboats had already tried this earlier, and had escaped with remarkably few losses. It would be a different matter with a fleet of slow, vulnerable transports and supply ships, but Grant felt the risk

ABOVE: The commander of the Vicksburg garrison was General John C. Pemberton. He had fought alongside Grant during the Mexican War.

was worth taking. The stakes were high, however, and he could have easily ended up with his army deep behind enemy lines, cut off from all means of resupply.

On the night of 16 April, three transports and eight gunboats slipped past Vicksburg, losing one transport for the 500 or so shots fired by the Confederates. Another six transports ran the gauntlet a few nights later, again losing one of their number. Meanwhile, Grant and two corps totalling some 23,000 men set off on the long trek through the Louisiana bayous, to the planned rendevous and crossing point at Hard Times, 20 miles below Vicksburg. To keep the Confederates pinned down in the town, he left Sherman to create a diversion to the north, while also launching cavalry raids against Pemberton's supply lines.

On 30 April, the Union army crossed the river unopposed, then chased 6000 confederates out of Port Gibson, just to the east of the crossing site. Grant immediately sent for Sherman, and within a few days he had around 40,000 men on the dry land on the rebels' side of the river. The forces against him were some 30,000, which did not give good odds for offen-

sive operations. However, the Confederate soldiers were scattered around in various independent detachments, so if he could engage them separately he could achieve local superiority in each case. His first worry was Joseph Johnston, who was forming an army at Jackson, the Mississippi state capital. This would endanger Grant's rear if he marched directly on Vicksburg, so he launched inland, planning for his troops to live off the land, extracting their food from the civilian farmers and villagers. On 14 May, Sherman's and McPherson's corps stormed into Jackson, routing the 7000 or so rebel troops there and wrecking everything of military or economic value in the town.

Pemberton was now greatly worried. His enemy had outflanked him in a brilliant maneuver, had demolished the army preparing to come to his aid, and was now about to march on the key fortress on the Mississippi. Still hoping for help from Johnston, he decided to try and delay Grant, and in a risky move marched eastward out of Vicksburg with over 23,000 men. On 16 May his troops clashed with those of McClernand and McPherson at Champion's Hill. Violent Union attacks, especially from

BELOW: The 8th Wisconsin Infantry fought at Vicksburg. They had an unusual mascot in the form of "Old Abe," a fully grown eagle that was carried on this specially made perch. "Old Abe" would soar skyward when the shooting started, and would fly back and forth above the battlefield until the fighting had stopped.

McPherson's corps, smashed against the Confederates for most of the day, eventually causing the men in grey to fall back, having suffered 3800 casualties. Worse was the fact that one whole division retreated away from Vicksburg toward the remnants of Johnston's army. The next day saw another attempt to stop Grant at Big Black River, but this time it was McClernand's men that shoved them aside. Greatly weakened, the demoralized troops retreated back to the fortifications at Vicksburg, with the prospect of a bitter siege in front of them.

By the 18th, Grant and Sherman stood on the heights overlooking Vicksburg, while their men deployed around the arc of trenches and emplacements constructed by the Confederate troops to defend the town. The Union soldiers had fought five successful battles in 17 days, and marched over 180 miles through some of the most difficult terrain imaginable. Their grueling campaign had completely swung the balance of the confrontation in their favor.

Grant wanted to keep the pressure on, not giving the enemy time to recover his morale or receive reinforcements. A general attack was ordered for the next day, without heavy artillery or engineering preparations. On the 19th, his three corps surged forward, charging in the open battle formations of the time. The defenders were well protected by a network of trenches, stockades and firing pits, covered by emplaced gun batteries firing from higher ground on the outskirts of the city. Withering fire from their rifled muzzle-loaders tore into the blue ranks and this first assault was quickly stopped in its tracks. Grant was anxious to win before the full blast of the summer heat took its toll, so he ordered another assault for three days time. While this was being prepared, the Union artillery began its bombardment of the town and its fortifications. The second assault managed to penetrate the outer trenchworks, but was eventually driven back, with Union forces suffering over 3200 casualties.

ABOVE: Once their initial attacks had failed, Grant's men settled down for a long siege, during which they constructed elaborate earthworks and gun positions.

RIGHT: An 1863
engraving showing the
fortifications and gun
batteries that defended
Vicksburg.

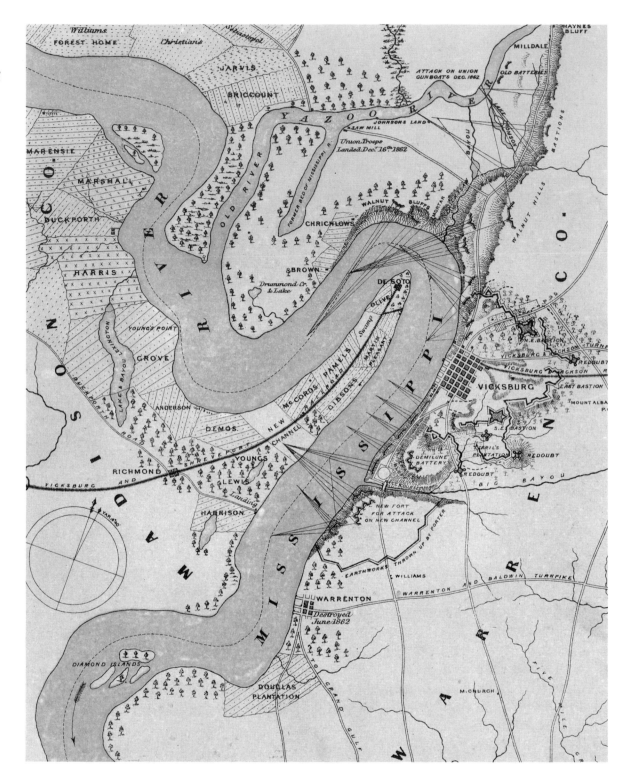

Grant realized that there was nothing else to do but settle down to a siege, that grim contest of will and stamina which so often rests on the resources of the quartermaster. Pemberton had sent out messengers to Johnston looking for help, and was prepared to wait while a relief force was formed. His couriers managed to get a message through the Union lines that he intended to hold "the most important point in the Confederacy," and its strategic position, "as long as possible." Once a regular "Old Army" officer, he was a loyal and energetic soldier with a strong concept of honor and integrity. Grant, who had known him during the Mexican war, had respect for him, stating that "This I thought of all the time he was in Vicksburg and I outside of it: and I knew he would hold on to the last."

Maybe Vicksburg was the most important point of the Confederacy, but Pemberton was to receive virtually no help from outside the fortress. Lincoln's strategy of engaging the Confederate armies at all points was paying off, and the rebels were fully committed elsewhere.

LEFT: Before the siege really took hold, there were numerous skirmishes in the woods around the city.

BELOW: The telegraph gave Civil War commanders much better knowledge of events outside their immediate span of control than in any previous war. This image shows the headquarters of Grant's signal corps just outside Vicksburg.

Johnston was the nearest senior commander with a reasonable sized force, but his reluctance to engage caused him to offer all forms of assistance short of actual help. Pemberton was on his own. His only other hope was that Grant's men would tire before the town's supplies ran out.

Through the summer weeks the siege tightened. Shelling from Grant's batteries and from the gunboats constantly rained down on the city, forcing the inhabitants to live a troglodyte existence in cellars, sewers and caves. Supplies of all kinds dwindled, while the Union troops dug sapping trenches toward the Confederate lines. Soldiers and civilians lived on reduced rations, causing many to suffer from dysentry and scurvy, while the rest were steadily becoming weaker and less able to fight. Morale steadily dropped as the cattle and horses were eaten, next came pets such as dogs and cats, and even skinned rats became a delicacy. All this time Grant was receiving reinforcements and re-supply from the river, a graphic illustration of the importance of the Mississippi. In late June, further pressure came from the Yankees as they tunneled under the Confederate lines, detonating huge mines and causing the starving defenders to use precious energy in restoring the breaches.

The steady erosion of his army made any attempt at a breakout futile, and eventually, after conferring with his generals, Pemberton had to face the inevitable. On 3 July he asked for an armistice and a meeting with Grant to discuss terms. The Union General wanted to finish the siege quickly, so he offered to parole the Confederate soldiers, an agreement where a man was set free in return for an oath not to bear arms until formally exchanged with other prisoners. This was an exceptionally good deal, although Grant had ulterior motives. He did

LEFT: Union engineers dug under the Confederate lines and blew a number of large craters, around which several vicious struggles took place.

not want the problem of transporting, feeding and guarding some 30,000 prisoners, and he may also have felt that such a large number of bitter, disillusioned and defeated men would be of more use spreading despondency back in their home towns and villages.

On 4 July 1863, after a siege of over 50 days, the Union troops marched into the city. Seeing the state of the starving defenders, many shared their rations, while others broke into and distributed the stores of profiteers and speculators who had been making huge profits from the misery of their compatriots. The Confederacy was effectively cut in half, with the Union able to control the Mississippi river along all its length. Grant was in no doubts as to the importance of the victory, writing "the fate of the Confederacy was sealed when Vicksburg fell." Pemberton was criticized by some for his surrender, with a few vocal southerners commenting on his northern birth, although Jefferson Davis placed the blame squarely on the shoulders of Johnston for not coming to his aid. As is often the case, those farthest from the scene of the action tended to make the most noise, it being much easier to criticize someone else for not choosing certain death by starvation or bullet than it is to face such a fate oneself.

ABOVE: *Nearly 30,000 soldiers and some 3000 civilians were trapped in the city. With no hope of rescue, starvation eventually forced surrender.*

RIGHT: *Foreign newspapers reported the war in lurid terms, often illustrated with "imaginative" scenes of battle. This artist has drawn the soldiers in European-style uniforms.*

IMPORTANT FROM AMERICA !!
Awful Slaughter at Vicksburg,
And Elsewhere,
The Bloody Conflict between the North & South

CONTINUED !

We regret to say that this unnatural war seems still to rush upon the unhappy Yanky with fearful impetuosity, so as to stun the entire population and saturate the States of America with blood, by sacrificing

well. They suffered terribly, for out of a regiment of 900, 600 were killed or wounded in an hour !

The Prize Court at Key West has laid down the law of confiscation so as to in-

demned at the rate of two each week."

Although 49,688 emigrants had arrived in New York from Ireland since the first of January, 1863, and though the negroes are said to be the best house-

line of works between the outer line supposed to be and the city. While the charge was being made on the 22nd acres of our sharpshooters, posted in the trees overlooking the fortifications, pushed in our contrabands and white men digging for dear life.

OUR LOSSES.
I regret to learn that Colonel Abbott, of the 20th Iowa, was killed on the 22nd instant. He was a brave officer, and his loss is universally regretted. In the battle of Champion's Hill, on the 16th, in-

that the Government will find in the Negroes effective supporters.

General Banks' loss from the 23rd to the 30th ult., was 1,080 men, including many of his oldest officers.

General Sherman has died of his wounds.

General Neal Dow is also dangerously wounded.

The Little Bighorn
1876

"I feel that my destiny is in the hands of the Almighty. This belief, more than any other facts or reason, makes me brave and fearless as I am."

GEORGE ARMSTRONG CUSTER

FAR RIGHT: *Taken just a few years before the Little Bighorn, this image shows Custer when he commanded the troops guarding the Pacific Railroad.*

BELOW: *A village on the Sioux reservation. The encampment attacked by the 7th Cavalry would have been similar to this, but with fewer women and children present.*

THE SHARP LITTLE action that took place around the Little Bighorn River on 25 June 1876 has become an American legend, inspiring more books, plays and films than almost any other battle. Yet this really was a tiny battle, with a few hundred dead and no great issue decided by its outcome. Nevertheless, the destruction of Major General George Armstrong Custer and his men caused such great outcry among the white American public that it gave the wars against the Native American Indian a new impetus which finally sealed the fate of the tribes.

A confederation led by the Sioux, Arapaho and Cheyenne had agreed to a treaty in 1868, which gave them reserved lands in North Dakota and Wyoming. In the following years, there was still friction and minor skirmishes along the borders of the Indian land, but real trouble only started when gold was discovered in the reservation. Thousands of prospectors flooded into the Black Hills, causing anger and frustration among the tribes, who in retaliation began to hunt and raid outside their own lands. The government declared such action illegal, and in 1876 various punitive actions were carried out by the frontier army.

One of these operations was led by Major General Alfred Terry, the Commandant of the Department of Dakota. A large hunting group

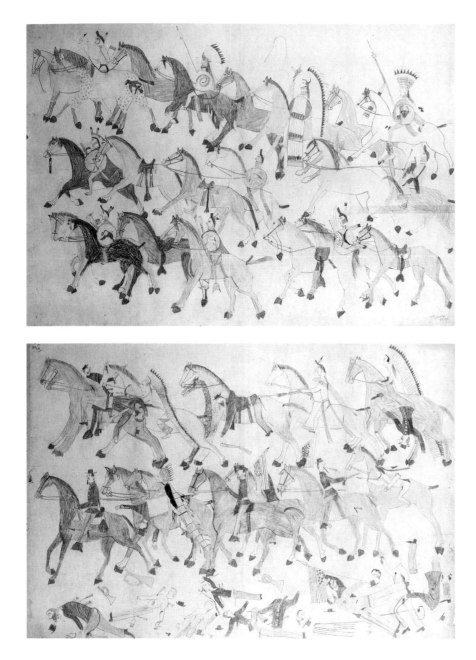

General George A. Custer, commanding 7th Cavalry

ABOVE: Drawn in 1881 by Red Horse, these images form part of a pictographic record of the Little Bighorn. The top painting shows Indian warriors charging toward the cavalry troopers while the lower depicts scenes from the battle.

of Sioux and Cheyenne braves was known to be in the wild area bounded by the Yellowstone River and the Bighorn Mountains, so Terry planned to search for them with 2500 men split into three columns; advancing from the east, west and south respectively. Terry himself commanded the eastern column, comprising over 900 men, the core of which was George Custer's 7th Cavalry. His estimate was that some 800 Indian warriors were in the area, but unknown to him, the usually independent-minded tribes had combined forces, and at least 1500 men were massed in one strong group under Chief Sitting Bull.

George Armstrong Custer was one of the most dashing and flamboyant officers in the army, a man who had earned a reputation for courage and quick-thinking during the Civil War and later Indian campaigns. He cut a spec-

tacular figure at the head of his regiment, with his long golden locks and dramatic black and gold uniforms that he designed himself. Custer was a determined self-publicist, making sure that stories of his exploits appeared in the eastern press to thrill an admiring public. Arrogance and disregard of any orders he disagreed with brought him into conflict with many of his seniors, while the harsh discipline he inflicted on those below caused resentment and dislike from his men. He had been promoted to Brevet Major General during the Civil War, but was now back to his substantive rank of Colonel – although most referred to him still as General. As the 1876 campaign began, he was smarting from yet another rebuke from the army authorities after unwisely meddling in politics, and this may have spurred him on in the hope of achieving a spectacular victory.

LEFT: *A modern watercolor of Custer, showing his flamboyant and idiosyncratic approach to military uniform.*

RIGHT: *Sitting Bull led the Sioux on the warpath after white prospectors entered their reservation in large numbers.*

RIGHT: A cavalry trooper wearing regulation issue blue jacket, gray breeches, high boots, wide-brimmed hat and leather gauntlets.

His command was the 7th Cavalry, one of the regiments that policed the wild frontier. Under Custer they had gained a reputation for being an efficient unit that could be relied upon to suppress insurrection, although they did this with great savagery, burning villages and hanging prisoners. There were weaknesses in the 7th Cavalry, however, especially in the poor relationships between Custer and some of his senior officers, including the second in command Major Marcus Reno and the Senior Captain, Frederick Benteen. With Custer, if a man was not a fawning hero-worshipper, then he was an enemy.

By June, Terry's column had joined up with the western detachment of 450 men led by Colonel John Gibbon. This combined force had been on the march for some time, when a reconnaissance party led by Major Reno discovered an Indian trail leading toward the Little Bighorn River. At about the same time, Terry's Crow scouts had seen smoke arising from the Little Bighorn Valley – it looked as if the war party had been found. On 21 June, Terry gave his orders. Custer was to lead his men up the River Rosebud, before swinging north into the Little Bighorn. In the meantime, Gibbon would move around to the north side and advance from the opposite direction,

Trooper

BELOW: A view of the plains on which Custer fought his last battle.

catching the Indians between the two forces. Gibbon would not be in place until the 26th, so it was vital that Custer remained out sight of the Indians until the planned time of attack, and in particular, he was ordered to avoid the trail previously discovered by Reno. As usual, George Custer had other ideas.

For three days Custer drove his men and horses forward in the heat of high summer, stopping only for a few hours rest at a time. On the 24th, he reached the trail discovered by Reno, and in flagrant breach of his orders, swung his troopers around to follow it. His march continued through the night, stopping for only a few hours as dawn broke to allow his Indian scouts to reconnoitre forward. They reported sightings of a large herd of Indian ponies, and numerous smoke trails rising from the Little Bighorn valley. As the morning progressed, the cavalry troopers realized that a number of Indians were now watching them from high ground, and that the element of surprise was lost. Custer was in a quandary. All the signals were that the Indian force was much larger than previously anticipated, but Gibbon's column would not be in position for another day. If the Indians broke camp and escaped into the mountains in response to Custer's appearance, the blame would be placed on him for disobeying his orders. His natural instinct was to attack immediately, and perhaps the thought of scoring a great coup without the help of others reinforced this inclination. Whatever the reason, he decided to lead his 450 men against an enemy whose precise location, deployment and strength was unknown.

Small detachments of US Cavalry had often defeated much larger groups of Indians by relying on their superior firepower and organization, so Custer's decision was not necessarily as reckless as it might seem. His fatal error at the Little Bighorn was to underestimate his enemy so much that he split his force into three separate detachments, each unable to support the other. Major Reno with three troops (112 men in total) was to cross the Little Bighorn river and advance up the valley to attack the Indian village from the south, while Captain Benteen was sent with another three troops to some high ground further to the south to prevent any Indians escaping in this direction. The main attack would be led by Custer, taking five troops (more than 200 men) along a high ridge to the northeast to ride around the Indian camp and attack it from the north.

ABOVE: Lieutenant James Calhoun was Custer's brother-in-law, and commanded "L" Troop. He and his men were killed alongside Custer. Some of the other officers who died with Custer are pictured throughout the chapter.

RIGHT: Custer's men carried single-shot Springfield carbines such as the one seen here. Many of their enemies had multi-shot magazine rifles.

BELOW: Lt. A. E. Smith commanded "E" Troop. His men tried to retreat down a steep ravine, but their way was blocked by the Indian warriors.

Lieutenant W. W. Cook

The first column to make contact was Reno's, and at around 1500 hours his three troops rode into the valley and into full view of the Indian tepees. At first he had the advantage of surprise, as the Indian Chiefs had not expected to be attacked by such a small force. This did not last, and within seconds Reno could see hundreds of braves rushing out of their camp toward him. He quickly realized the peril his men were now in and ordered them to dismount and form a skirmishing line. The 7th cavalry were trained to fight on foot, and Reno's men started an accurate fire with their single-shot Springfield carbines. The Indians still worked their way forward though, pushing the bluecoats back to the east where they took cover in a small clump of trees. The soldiers were shocked by the amount and quality of gunfire coming their way. Expecting the native warriors to be armed with traditional weapons such as bows and axes, it was a nasty surprise to find over a third of the braves equipped with Winchester repeating rifles superior to their own Springfields.

It rapidly became obvious that Reno's men could not survive long where they were, and that their only chance lay in getting back across the river to the high ground to the east. A desperate running battle ensued, with the Indians intermingled with the cavalrymen in a confused rush for a fordable point on the Little Bighorn. As they reached the river, the men had to force their horses over six-foot high banks, crashing into the water as the Indian shots and arrows rained down on them. Eventually they managed to stumble up the steep bluff on the other side and catch their breath while they prepared for another Indian attack. 32 troopers were known to be dead, 7 were wounded and another 15 were missing.

While this was going on, Custer led his column of five troops along the high ridge to the northeast of the camp. He had seen the start of Reno's attack, which caused him to send a messenger back for more ammunition, but he still seems to have been confident of the final outcome. As they came within sight of the village, a large force of warriors was sent by

Chief Crazy Horse to block Custer's descent. Working their way up the ridge using any available cover, the Indians soon stopped Custer's progress, bringing his men under accurate and heavy fire. The troopers were now dismounted and firing back, but their enemies outgunned them, both in the accuracy and quantity of fire.

Custer's column was spread out over the hillside, with each of the five troops forming its own little nest of resistance. From Indian accounts, it seems that their warriors tried a number of mounted charges which the bluecoats managed to repel. Two troops may have attempted a breakout down a steep ravine to

LEFT: *Another view of the same scene, with the flag still flying and Custer almost the last man on his feet.*

Lieutenant J. J. Critenden

Lieutenant J. G. Sturgis

the west, but this was quickly blocked by the Indians. By now most of the 7th's horses were dead, shot by their riders so that the carcasses could provide some cover on the bare rocky hillside. It was all to no avail. Each little pocket of resistance was snuffed out one by one, and after an hour every one of the 200 or so cavalrymen was dead, with the Indians scalping the bodies and carrying off weapons and uniforms as trophies. The soldiers had fought to the last, earning grudging respect from their enemies. "They kept in order and fought like brave warriors as long as they had a man left," was the Crow Chief's verdict.

As Custer's men breathed their last, Reno had been joined by the remainder of the regiment under Benteen. The two men argued over the best course of action, while the sound of shooting could be heard from over the hills. Reno felt that his men were too shattered by their escape and unable to ride back toward the battle, but some of the younger officers disagreed, leading their men into the valley toward the sound of the guns. They very quickly came up against a large body of Indians and had to make a hasty escape back toward Reno. They were chased by the braves, and the cavalrymen on the hill had to withstand a num-

Lieutenant W. Van W. Reilly

Lieutenant J. E. Porter

ber of desperate attacks on their position, losing another 18 men and 43 wounded. The remnants of the 7th spent an uncomfortable night on the exposed hillside, although nineteen volunteers managed to fill the water canteens from the River Bighorn. The next day the Indians made two further determined attacks, but that afternoon they broke camp and moved off toward the mountains.

The 7th had lost nearly 300 men, including every one of those that rode with Custer. Indian casualties had been much lighter, the best estimates being between 60 and 70 dead. In the long term, Custer's last stand had more symbolic importance than military effect. The more thoughtful of the Indian Chiefs realized that such a victory would spur the white man to seek revenge and would never be forgiven. Many tribes dispersed, some crossing into Canada to avoid retribution as the army came looking for them in much greater strength than before. Never again would the tribes take to the warpath in this manner.

While most of the survivors of the 7th were regarded as heroes, Reno became the target of whisper and rumor, much of it promoted by Custer's coterie of supporters. The slander became so strong that he eventually requested a Court of Inquiry into his conduct, although even this came back with only faint praise. He became an embittered and lonely man, and was eventually court-martialed for disciplinary offenses and drunkenness. His men had a rather different opinion of his conduct, however, as just one week after the battle they sent a petition to Congress praising his steadfastness and requesting that he and Benteen be promoted. Congress turned them down.

ABOVE: "Comanche," the only survivor of Custer's column, later became a Regimental mascot.

Lieutenant H. M. Harrington

Rorke's Drift

1879

". . . they tried to leap the parapets, and at times seized our bayonets, only to be shot down. Looking back, one cannot but admire their fanatical bravery."

COLOUR SERGEANT FRANK BOURNE

THE WAR BETWEEN Great Britain and the Zulu nation of 1879 was largely the product of one man's paranoia and ambition. Sir Henry Bartle Frere, the British High Commissioner in South Africa, was convinced of the threat to his territories posed by the Zulu army. Believing that King Cetewayo's regiments would attack into Natal at the first opportunity, his response was to find a way of sending British soldiers into Zululand in a pre-emptive attack. By manipulation and machination he managed to take advantage of various political disputes, until he had sufficient excuse to launch his invasion.

BELOW: *King Cetewayo of the Zulus controlled a uniquely militarized society, the fear of which prompted the British invasion of his country.*

The government in London was less than pleased, but by the time they realized what was going on it was too late to stop the attack. 6000 regular and colonial troops, supplemented by 9000 levied natives marched across the Natal border into Zululand, divided into three separate columns under the command of Lieutenant General Lord Chelmsford. He himself traveled with the third column, which comprised two battalions of the 24th Regiment, a regiment of the Natal Native Contingent (NNC), small detachments of Natal volunteer cavalry and a battery of Royal Artillery. On 11 January 1879, this column crossed the Mzinyathi River into Zululand, leaving an advanced supply dump and hospital at the point where they forded the river – a place called Rorke's Drift.

A former trading post and now a mission station, Rorke's Drift was an isolated homestead comprising two brick and stone buildings with thatched roofs. One had been a house, but was now in use as a field hospital, while the other was being used as a store for army supplies, mainly large wooden boxes of biscuits and meat, and sacks of maize (known locally as "mealies"). The two buildings sat some 40 yards apart, and there were a small cookhouse and outbuildings further away, together with a stone-walled cattle pen or "kraal." Guarding this position was the responsibility of B Company of the 2nd Battalion, the 24th Regiment, one of the "new style" battalions that recruited largely from one part of Britain. B Company's soldiers were mainly from Wales and Gloucestershire, with a few from other parts of the country. There was also a detachment of Royal Engineers at Rorke's Drift, while the hospital held 30 or so men from the other units of Chelmsford's column. To supplement B Company, there was a large company of the NNC, poor quality native levies led by a dubious variety of white officers and NCOs.

The senior officer present was Major Henry Spalding, with Assistant Commissary Dunne in charge of the stores and with Acting Assistant Commissary Dalton as his second. B Company was under the temporary command of Lieutenant Gonville Bromhead, a 33-year-old professional who, while lacking dazzling brilliance, was a mature and competent officer. The Royal Engineer detachment was led by Lieutenant John Chard, who was a year younger than Bromhead but with more seniority. The infantrymen of B Company were relatively young, but they had gained a fair amount of combat experience in their year in Africa.

In 1879 they still wore bright red uniform tunics topped by a large white cork helmet, although most had toned down the helmet with various improvised dyes of tea, coffee or mud. Their weapon was the Martini-Henry rifle, a single shot weapon which fired a hefty .45in bullet 1700 yards, although it was most effec-

tive from about 400 yards. Brass cartridges were fed into the breech one at a time, and a trained man could fire an aimed shot every few seconds. Each rifle could also be fitted with an 18-inch socket bayonet, a narrow pointed weapon which would spear a man with ease.

On 20 January 1879, there was nothing to suggest that the day would not be another quiet one at Rorke's Drift. Chelmsford's column was known to be camped a few miles over the hills at Isandhlwana, intending to search toward the central expanse of Zululand. Spalding was expecting more troops to pass through the Drift on their way forward, and he rode back down the track to meet them, leaving Chard in command of the post with the parting words, ". . . of course, nothing will happen." When gunfire was heard from over the hills, little thought was given to it, although three men, including the Swedish owner of the post, climbed up the nearby Shiyane (or Oskarberg) mountain to see

ABOVE: Zulu headmen in 1881. They carry the short stabbing assegai and the shorter version of the cowhide shield. Most of this ceremonial dress would not be worn on campaign.

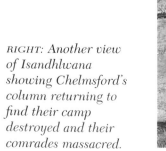

ABOVE: *A view of the Battle of Isandhlwana, when nearly 20,000 Zulus surprised the 1300 men left in the camp.*

RIGHT: *Another view of Isandhlwana showing Chelmsford's column returning to find their camp destroyed and their comrades massacred.*

if they could catch a glimpse of Chelmsford. The placid calm of the afternoon was shattered, however, when a few panic-stricken horsemen rode into the post, telling of a great disaster.

While Chelmsford and half his force had been out searching ahead of the rest, 20,000 Zulus had swept on to his camp, wiping out the 1300 defenders in a savage two-hour battle. The few survivors who had reached Rorke's Drift were panicky and incoherent, but the gist of their story was clear – the Zulus had won an overwhelming victory, and were likely to be heading this way.

Chard and Bromhead immediately considered their options. They could try and run, hoping that the Zulus would not chase them too far into Natal. This was discounted, as there were 30 or so patients in the hospital, about nine of whom could only be carried on carts. These would limit the speed of the evacuation such that the Zulus were bound to catch up, forcing the British to fight against overwhelming odds in the open. Their best chance of survival was to try and fortify the post and fight it out where they were. Acting Assistant Commissary Dalton suggested using the stores to create

barricades, and at about 1530 hours the troops set to work with a will, manhandling the 200 pound mealie bags and 110 pound ration boxes in the blistering heat. A wall was built across the rear of the post, joining the hospital and the store. This was based around the two ox wagons, which were reinforced by ration boxes and mealie bags. Another wall of mealie bags joined the two buildings along the front of the post, creating a defensive compound of sorts. Loopholes were knocked in the walls of the buildings to cover all directions of approach.

While this was going on, more refugees from Isandhlwana trickled past, including a contingent of Natal horse. Their panic spread to the NNC Company, who, along with most of their officers and NCOs, suddenly ran down the track to Helpmakaar, leaving one officer and a few corporals at their post. The defenders were now down to less than 140 men, and Chard, worried that he would not be able to hold the whole perimeter, ordered another wall to be built between the buildings, dividing the compound into two.

A few miles away, the men that were approaching Rorke's Drift were the products of

ABOVE: This view of the fighting at Isandhlwana shows details of the uniforms and firearms of the British Army in Zululand.

a uniquely militarized African society, one which had taken shape under King Shaka less than a hundred years earlier. The Zulu King commanded the allegiance of many clans, whose young men had to serve a number of years in the King's service until freed to marry and live their own lives. The men, serving in guilds or "ambutho," lived in barrack-style villages and acted as hunters, policemen, and in times of war, soldiers. Each guild was formed of men of a particular age and fought as a regiment, gaining in seniority as they grew older. Once they had reached the age of around 40, they would be freed by the King from their obligation to serve, and their regiment would be disbanded. They fought and traveled light, each man wearing only a loincloth, and a simple headdress to identify his regiment, and carrying an oval cowskin shield and a number of spears or assegai for throwing or stabbing. Many of the men that attacked Rorke's Drift also carried firearms, but these were a mixture of obsolete and poorly maintained weapons of various calibers and questionable effectiveness.

King Cetewayo had not intended to follow up his victory at Isandhlwana with a sortie into Natal, fearing that such an invasion would provoke a much stronger British response. Unfortunately, many of his troops were frustrated at having seen little of the Isandhlwana action, especially the three regiments who had been sent to cover the right flank. When they reached the Mzinyatha River, they barely hesitated before pouring across and heading toward Rorke's Drift. The first to arrive, however, were actually from a fourth regiment, the 500 men of the iNdluyengwe who had been chasing fugitives from the earlier battle.

At around 1630 hours, Private Hitch, who was posted on the roof of the storehouse, let out a shout of warning – the Zulus were in sight. As the British scrambled into position, a line of men appeared over the shoulder of Shiyane, skirmishing toward the rear of the post using the cover provided by rocks and shrubs. They started to shoot as they came forward, but with little result. The redcoats held their fire until the Zulus were within 500 yards, then took carefully aimed shots at the approaching figures. The Martini-Henry was remarkably accurate at 400 yards, and it was at this distance that their shots began to tell. The Zulus kept moving forward though, getting to within 50 yards of the rear wall before being forced to take cover in a ditch and in some brush behind the small cookhouse.

The attack then swung to the left, going around to the front of the hospital, where the wall was much weaker and where there were less defenders able to shoot. It was here that the first hand-to-hand struggles took place, with Zulus stabbing at the soldiers with their short assegais, but in turn being shot or run through by the redcoats. The Martini-Henry and its bayonet gave an infantryman a reach of over six feet, and would slice through the thin shield carried by the Zulus.

It was at about 1640 hours that the main body of Zulus arrived to join in the attack. Three regiments led by Prince Dabulamanzi attacked the north side of the hospital, with the older

FAR LEFT: De Neuville's dramatic painting of the action at Rorke's Drift is inaccurate in that it shows the evacuation of the hospital taking place before the yard was abandoned.

BELOW: An engraving of the scene in front of the Rorke's Drift post the morning after the battle.

ABOVE: *The relief force from the Mounted Infantry arriving on the morning of the 23rd. The cattle kraal, mealie bag redoubt and burnt-out hospital can all be clearly seen.*

men of the renowned uThulwana in the lead. There were now some 4500 Zulus, too many to attack at once, so men lay in the undergrowth waiting their turn to charge the barricades. The Zulus would come forward in a series of rushes, using what cover was available in an attempt to get to grips with the defenders. The British responded with fearsome volleys of rifle fire then the bayonet. While this was going on, long range fire was dropping into the compound from the rear, coming from Zulus who had been stationed on a terrace at the foot of Shiyane. Although not particularly accurate, this fire still caused some casualties and forced the British to detail some riflemen to fire back.

For the next hour the attacks continued, with the Martinis growing painfully hot, their recoil creating agonizing bruises on the shoulders. Non-combatants like Surgeon Reynolds and Chaplain Smith distributed ammunition and water, as did the walking wounded. Chard, Bromhead and Colour Sergeant Frank Bourne continually rushed to areas of the wall that were hard-pressed, leading small groups of men to strengthen that section. By about 1800 hours Chard was worried about the continuing pres-

sure and ordered his men to pull back to the storehouse, behind the wall he had built across the compound. This meant that the Zulus could now come right up to the walls and cover the compound with fire. There were still men fighting inside the hospital who were now cut off from the rest of the force, but they would have to survive as best they could. Chard wanted another fall-back position should the enemy get into the storehouse, so Dunne began struggling with the remaining mealie bags to build a circular redoubt in front of the building.

The Zulus now forced their way into the hospital, which became the scene of a truly desperate little struggle. As the thatched roof caught fire, the men inside shot and stabbed at the attackers, fighting in the doorways and windows of the building. As Private Henry Hook wrote, the fire "put us in a terrible plight, because it meant that we were either to be massacred or burnt alive." Many of the rooms were not connected, and the British had to knock holes through the brick and clay walls to retreat through the building. The sick and wounded were passed through these gaps by able-bodied soldiers, while others just about managed to hold off the frantic attacks. Even so some of the wounded were stabbed to death where they lay. Eventually the survivors staggered into the courtyard, where they had to run the gauntlet of spears and bullets as they made for the storehouse. Fire from their comrades helped protect them, but at least one man died during this perilous journey.

It was now dark, and the flames from the hospital cast a ghastly flickering light over the scene, helping the British riflemen pick their targets on that side of the post. From about 1930 hours the Zulus shifted their attack to the east, where they were not illuminated by the fire. They managed to take control of the stone cattle pen, but still could not get across the barricades. It was about now that the defenders first realized that the attacks were getting less frequent, with gaps of 10 or 15 minutes between each assault. Hopes of survival increased as by 2200 hours the Zulus were reduced to sporadic flurries of shooting, and by 0200 hours they had disappeared from sight.

Dawn brought a fearful scene, as the weary, smoke-blackened soldiers looked over the bodies spread in front of them, wondering if the Zulus had gone for good. At around 0700 hours it seemed as if the nightmare was about to begin again, as a vast host of Zulus appeared on the hills to the southwest. They looked down on the post for a few minutes, then to the amazement of the defenders they withdrew from sight. The reason shortly became ap-

parent when Chelmsford and a column of troops (those that had been away from the camp at Isandhlwana) rode into view, surveying the dead Zulus, smouldering wreckage and cheering troopers with amazement.

The Battle of Rorke's Drift was a tiny aside to the disaster of Isandhlwana, but one which the Victorian public were to latch onto as an example of• British pluck overcoming the savage hordes. Eleven Victoria Crosses were awarded, the most given for any one action in British Army history. Chard and Bromhead were recipients, as were Reynolds, Dalton and Corporal Schiess of the NNC. Fifteen men had been killed, with two more dying later from their wounds. There were 15 seriously wounded and almost every man had minor cuts, bruises and grazes of some kind. The Zulus had suffered terribly, and the best estimate is that 600 died and another 400 were seriously wounded. The uThulwana had been destroyed as a fighting force, while the other regiments were shamed by their failure to take such a small outpost. Cetewayo was also horrified by the casualties inflicted on his men, 600 by the defenders of Rorke's drift and 3-4000 by those who died at Isandhlwana. If all British soldiers fought like this, then how could he win when they came again in greater force? Six months later his question was answered in the negative, when Chelmsford returned and finally defeated the Zulu nation at Ulundi. Sir Henry Frere had achieved his objective.

BELOW: A photograph of B Company taken some time after the battle. It is difficult to identify individuals, but Colour Sergeant Frank Bourne can be seen on the extreme left.

Khartoum
1884

"What I have to do is to submit my will to His, however bitter may be the events which happen to me."

GENERAL CHARLES GORDON

BELOW: *This portrait captures something of the almost Messianic expression noted in Gordon by many of his contemporaries.*

ON 19 FEBRUARY 1884 in Khartoum, hundreds of excited citizens and soldiers gathered around a tall, smooth-faced Englishman as he disembarked from a river steamer. The legendary and revered General Gordon, soldier, missionary and visionary, had come to save them from the wild rebels that threatened their city. His first words may have caused the more thoughtful to pause though, "I come without soldiers, but with God on my side, to redress the evils of the Sudan."

Gordon had been sent to Khartoum by a reluctant British government in an effort to get them out of trouble with as little effort and expenditure as possible. At that time Sudan was under occupation by a corrupt and inefficient Egyptian colonial administration, one which supported Sudanese slave traders and milked the countryside and people for all they could get. Egypt herself also had to put up with a high level of interference from foreign powers, as her inability to repay international debts had caused many institutions to be taken over by Europeans. Britain had the greatest interest, and many administrators and soldiers were seconded to Egypt to improve the efficiency of the government and the military.

Sudan was a fertile ground for the seeds of revolution, and in the 1860s one man emerged who was able to combine the many groups of dissaffected Sudanese into one powerful force. Mohammed Ahmed Ibn al-Sayid Abdullah claimed to be a descendant of the prophet Mohammed, and taking the name of the "Mahdi" or "Guided One" soon began to preach a doctrine of austerity, nationalism and total religious dedication. The sect he joined, and soon came to lead, were known as the Summaniya Dervish, and they quickly took control of large areas of the wild, rocky desert that made up most of Sudan. From about 1881 his men successfully routed the contingents of Egyptian and Sudanese troops sent to suppress them, including the column led by the British General Hicks. By 1884, it was feared that the Mahdi's forces were in a position to threaten the Sudanese capital, Khartoum, whose nervous population of Egyptian colonists, Sudanese colonial officials and ordinary Sudanese appealed to Egypt and Britain for help.

In London, Gladstone's administration were reluctant to get involved in another colonial campaign, especially in defense of the corrupt Egyptian government and their slave traders.

Their hope was that the population of Khartoum could be evacuated, with the minimum cost to the British taxpayer. They wanted to send a figurehead to Khartoum, someone who had the strength of character to organize an evacuation but who could also gain the confidence of the Sudanese. There was really only one choice; the hero of China, the man who had already been Governor-General of Sudan, the darling of the Victorian press – General Charles Gordon.

The exact terms of his mission have since been shrouded in obfuscation, but it appears that he was sent with instructions to do what he could to protect the people of Khartoum. The government said later that he had been given explicit instructions to organize an evacuation, and told in no uncertain terms that no British military help would be forthcoming. Others disputed this, insisting that Gordon had been misled into believing that there would be assistance if needed. Whatever the truth, he was appointed Governor-General of Sudan by a grateful Egyptian ruler, and arrived in Khartoum on 19 February, accompanied by his aide-de-camp, Colonel J. D. H. Stewart.

Charles Gordon was a complex character whose fundamental Christianity and strong sense of personal duty had often led him into brushes with his military and political superiors. A military engineer, he had gained his reputation during the wars in China and in earlier postings to Central Africa and Sudan. Energetic, but with an unworldly manner (he could never manage money, tending to give it away as soon as he had any), he had the ability to inspire confidence in those he led, although by the time of his Khartoum mission his behavior had become decidedly erratic.

When he took the reins of government at Khartoum, he was painfully aware of the weakness of the Egyptian position. He set about creating stronger defenses for the city, paying arrears in wages to his troops, releasing prisoners and putting the administration on a more organized footing. In the first months he sent a

ABOVE: There was great excitement among the citizens of Khartoum when the hero of China and the Sudan arrived, as they thought, to save their city.

ABOVE: *Gordon's forces managed to undertake a series of raids and sorties, often using armed river steamers.*

with them, was an impossible task. He announced this in telegrams to Cairo, while promising the occupants of Khartoum that a British relief force would come to their rescue. Showing a much more pragmatic attitude than his superiors, he also tried to deal with the Mahdi and local tribes. These negotiations failed, and he realized that it was only a matter of time before the city was surrounded. On 12 March, a large army of Dervish warriors camped a few miles from the outer defenses of the city – the siege of Khartoum had begun.

Gordon's fighting force had originally started at some 25,000, but desertion had already weakened this somewhat. His troops were regular Egyptian and Sudanese soldiers, along with a few thousand irregulars from various parts of North Africa. The only European officers were himself, Stewart and Frank Powers, a man who fulfilled the dual role of British Consul and correspondent for *The Times.* Khartoum itself sat at the junction of the White and Blue Nile, and the city was bounded by the river on the north side. A number of simple earthen forts sat alongside the river to the east and west, joined by a line of trenches curving south in an arc from the Blue Nile's banks in the east, to those of the White Nile in the west. A strong fort sat at Omdurman, on the west bank of the White Nile, which was garrisoned by some 250 men.

There was little in the way of heavy weapons and equipment, but Gordon used his engineering skills to the utmost in preparing his defense. His collection of 12 guns of varying types was distributed along his trench lines, while thousands of improvised land-mines were laid. Made from such items as biscuit boxes, these were filled with explosive and packed with nails, bullets and any other scrap metal, rigged to detonate by trip wire. Improvisation was also a feature of Khartoum's naval force, seven river steamers which had metal plates attached to their hulls and were each armed with a 9-pounder gun.

Passive resistance was not Gordon's style, and he soon set a pattern of aggressive sorties by his garrison, although on one occasion a strong attack by over 1000 of his men was betrayed by two Sudanese officers. His relationship with his army was somewhat ambivalent, in that he had total scorn for his irregulars and the Egyptians (who he normally referred to as "hens"), but he did have an affection for the Sudanese. While a strong Christian, he had a sneaking admiration for confirmed be-

few thousand civilians down the Nile on his small fleet of river steamers, but realized that such a method was inadequate to deal with the 34,000 people in the city. As reports came in of the build up of the Mahdi's forces he realized that evacuation across the desert terrain, with only the food and water that could be carried

lievers of other religions, and especially for the austere desert lifestyle of the Mahdi and his warriors.

The besieging force was under the command of one of the Mahdi's most senior Emirs, the experienced and renowned Wad el-Nejumi. His Dervish warriors (or *ansars*) were mainly armed with traditional spears and cross-handled broadswords, wearing only light linen tunics and trousers, with no other protection. Some had rifles scavenged from earlier battlefields, but few were skilled in their use. The Dervishes were renowned for their courage in the attack, pressing forward on numerous occasions into the massed fire of breech-loading rifles, and had swept away Egyptian and Sudanese troops on many battlefields. One of the most martial tribes was the Hadendowah, and it was their method of wearing their hair in a wild spray that caused their nickname of "Fuzzy-Wuzzy" among British troops.

On 5 May, Gordon heard that the Mahdi had taken Berber, which meant that telegraph and river communications with higher authority were now cut. Shells were now falling sporadically on the city from the small collection of Dervish artillery, while the sound of constant drumming from the enemy camp echoed over the trenches. Despite this, the siege was never total, and messengers were able to make the hazardous journey into and out of Khartoum many times over the next few months.

Gordon did what he could to keep morale high. He sent his steamer force on foraging expeditions up river, where they often exchanged fire with groups of Dervishes. He also created his own system of decorations and medals for his troops, having them made from stocks of metal and ribbon in the city. He created his own currency and tried to prevent food hoarding and speculation, although this was never totally successful. He also left the gates open to anyone who wanted to leave, stating that if anyone would rather support the Mahdi then they were better out of the city. Conversely, he was reluctant to banish anyone from Khartoum, and many who resented the British and Egyptian presence stayed to benefit from the food supplies within the city.

Back in Britain, the government were horrified to realize that the great hero was not going to get them out of a jam after all, and that pressure was building to send troops to relieve Khartoum. A barrage of messages had come from Gordon asking for such a relief force, some making wild suggestions about request-

ing the Turks or the French to provide troops. Gladstone had tried to wash his hands of the business, saying that Gordon was not his responsibility, that he had exceeded his orders, or even that Gordon could still get out himself. It became apparent that public sympathy had swung behind the lonely soldier, staying at his post when all others had abandoned him, and that something must be done. Reluctantly and after much foot dragging, a relief force was ordered to go to his rescue, to be led by the best known general in Britain, Sir Garnet Wolseley.

On 9 September, British soldiers disembarked in Egypt, although it would be another month before they set off on overcrowded steamboats on a slow and difficult trip through the largely uncharted waters of the Nile. In the meantime, Gordon had sent Stewart, Powers and the French Consul in one of his precious steamers in a desperate attempt to find a relieving force, but when their boat ran aground they were murdered by Mahdist tribesmen.

BELOW: Sir Garnet Wolseley, who commanded the relief operation, was regarded as the most skilled and progressive general the British then had.

436 108

Decr 13 we thought he was killed by the noise
he made, in his fall. Arabs fire their Krupp
continually into town, from South front, but we
now takes any notice of it; the Arabs at Goba, only
fired one shell at Palace today, which burst in
air.

Decr 14. Arabs fired 2 shells at Palace this morning.
546 ardebs Dhoora! in store, also 83,525 okes of
Biscuit! 10.30 A.M. the steamers are down at
ondaroman, engaging the Arabs. consequently I am
on tenter hooks! 11.30 A.M. steamers returned, the
"Bordeen" was struck by a shell in her battery, we
had only one man wounded, ————————— 20 person.
We are going to send down "Bordeen" tomorrow with
this journal. If I was in command of the 200
men of Expeditionary Force, which are all that
are necessary for moment, I should stop just
below Halfyeh & attack Arabs at that place
before I came on here to Kartoum. I should
then communicate with North Fort, and act
—————— according to circumstances. I now mark
this, if Expeditionary Force, and I ask for no more
than 200 men does not come in 10 days, the
town may fall, and I have done my best for
the honor of our country. Good bye

C. E. Gordon.

You send me no information
though you have lots of
money. C.G.

As the months wore on, conditions in Khartoum were deteriorating and food was scarce. Gordon himself was becoming more strident in his pleas, claiming (with some justification) that he had been betrayed. He also talked more and more of martyrdom, developing a fatalistic view of his future, almost as if death would be welcome. The population were becoming restive, disbelieving his reassurances that the British would not abandon them. Many felt they had a better chance outside, and a constant trickle defected to the Mahdist lines. By November, people were dying from starvation, with the survivors too exhausted to bury the bodies. A few speculators continued to hoard food and sell at fantastic prices, while others stole from the small stocks still held by the city government. Dysentry spread quickly, weakening the troops holding the line and causing gaps to form in the trenches. There was now only some 8000 armed men in the line, and a good proportion of them were too weak or sick to fight effectively. During this time Gordon became a lonely, rather distant figure, spending hours at the upper windows of the Governor's Palace with his telescope, looking for signs of a relief column.

The enemy lines came closer through December and January, and the Dervishes launched a series of attacks on the fortification at Omdurman, which ended in the surrender of that fort. It was now even harder to get messengers out of the city, and a good many of those who tried were captured. By January, Wolseley's relief column had also struggled up the Nile to Korli, where he landed nearly 2000 men to form the "Desert Column" under Brigadier General Sir Herbert Stewart. The river swung from here in a great loop north before curving down to Khartoum, but by cutting across the base of this loop a land force would only have to travel some 200 miles.

Guardsmen, Hussars and Mounted Infantry had been hastily trained to ride camels, and accompanied by a few supply wagons, light artillery and a Gardiner machine gun, they set off on a hard journey, through empty terrain with little water. Progress was slow, and on 17 January they were intercepted by 10,000 Dervish warriors at the wells of Abu Klea. The British soldiers formed a single square, in which two ranks of men stood shoulder to shoulder facing outward, with the camels and wagons in the center. They were equipped with

FAR LEFT: The last message received from Gordon. It ends, "if the expeditionary force, and I ask for no more than 200 men, does not come in 10 days, then the town may fall, and I have done my best for the honour of our Country. Good bye."

BELOW: The river expedition to relieve Khartoum had to negotiate numerous rapids and cataracts.

the breach-loading Martini-Henry rifle, from which they could fire one shot every few seconds. Constant volley fire devastated the tribesmen as they charged, although there was a tense few minutes when some managed to burst through one corner of the square into the middle. Disaster was averted by the mass of camels which hindered the Dervishes once inside the square, and by the rear ranks on the opposite side of the square, who cooly turned about and fired into the confused mass. Within ten minutes the battle was over. The British lost only 86 men, whereas over 1000 Dervishes lay strewn around their square. The next day the column continued its march.

On the 21st, they came to the Nile, where they met four of Gordon's steamers which had been sent to find them. General Stewart had been killed in a skirmish at Abu Kru, so command had devolved upon Colonel Charles Wilson, who now took a small party upstream in the boats, toward Khartoum. Back in the city, the coming of winter had caused the level of the river to drop, which exposed new ground near the banks and created gaps in Gordon's defenses. Messengers had informed both Gordon and the Mahdi of the result of Abu Klea and of the approach of the Desert Column, and both must have known that the critical hour was near

On 25 January, the Mahdi launched his men in a general assault, yelling praises to Mohammed and Allah as they charged into Gordon's trench line. They swamped over the weakened troops in a number of places, and a series of short but bloody struggles took place. To the west, the shrinking river had left a 150 yard stretch of mud which was undefended, and Wad-el-Nejumi led his troops across this and into the city itself. The defenses had been cracked wide open, and the Mahdists poured into Khartoum, slaughtering the defenders and most of the civilians they came across. Gordon is supposed to have waited calmly at his palace, offering no resistance as he was speared by a blood-crazed Dervish. Another account has him fighting to the last with revolver and sword, and this seems more likely in view of his history. Within hours the battle became a slaughter, as the victorious warriors rampaged through the city, killing and looting.

Two days later Wilson and the steamboats hove into view, shocked to see no flag flying from the palace and Dervishes shooting at them from the ramparts. There was nothing else to do now but turn back and take the troops home. The fall of Khartoum caused an immense stir in Britain, with popular (and Royal) feelings running high against the government. The British had been effectively ejected from Sudan; a severe blow to Imperial pride. The Mahdi did not enjoy the fruits of his victory either, as within six months he followed Gordon to the grave, killed by illness. His successor would rule for some 15 years until the British returned in strength to take back Sudan.

LEFT: *After Khartoum was retaken by the British in 1898, a memorial service was held to honor the memory of Gordon.*

BELOW: *Gordon's body was never found, although his severed head is said to have been brought to Rudolf Slatin, an Austrian who was at that time a prisoner of the Mahdi.*

BOTTOM: *Once Wilson's relief force found that Khartoum had fallen, they had to make a long and dangerous journey back to Abu Klea. Losing their steamers to hostile action, they had to be rescued themselves by another steamer, commanded by Captain Beresford.*

ON BOARD THE "FAFIEH."   COPYRIGHT.   MADAME TUSSAUD & SONS EXHIBITION.

Peking

1900

"It will be seen that I was acting under orders and I think that anyone must have done as I did."

CAPTAIN LEWIS HALLIDAY VC

CHINA IN 1900 was a paper tiger, weakened by internal schism and preyed upon by foreign governments who interfered in her trade, politics and society. This meddling was such that the removal of foreign influence became a powerful desire of many Chinese, including the secret society known as the Boxers. Religious fanatics, the members of this group practiced secret gymnastic and fighting routines which they believed would have spiritual and magical effects, and bestow invulnerability in battle. It was these routines that were mistaken for boxing by westerners, giving the society its common name.

The Boxers had been carrying out attacks on Chinese Christians and foreign missionaries for some years, but recent encouragement from within the Imperial Court had caused a dramatic increase. The Dowager Empress Tz'u Hsi was playing a devious game against westernizers and reformers among her royal rivals, and in support of this she tacitly encouraged the Boxers. The main group of foreigners in Peking lived and worked in the Legation area, a separate district sandwiched between the Imperial City and the great wall which marked the edge of the Tartar City. Over 500 Europeans, Japanese and Americans lived here, and con-

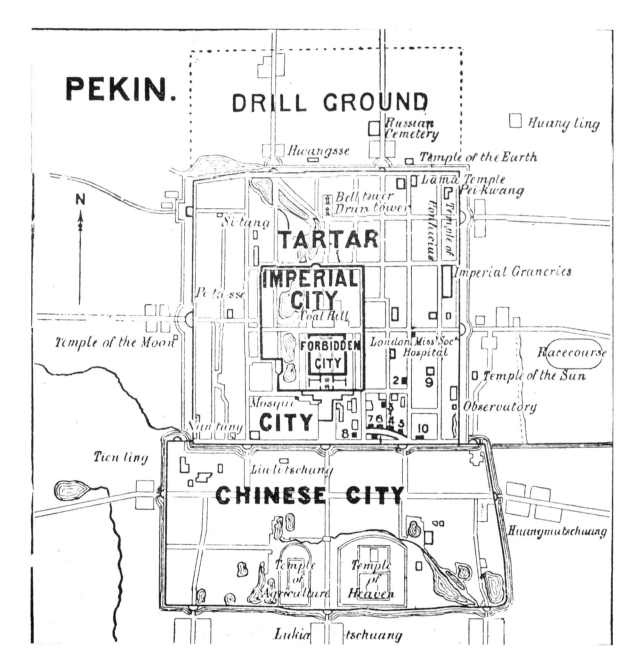

stant anti-foreign propaganda and threats had them fearing for their lives.

The French Minister took the initiative of asking for guards to be sent from the foreign warships off the coast at Taku, 100 miles to the southeast. His request was answered by a small multi-national group of soldiers comprising 78 British Royal Marines, 75 Russians, 25 Austrians, 50 United States Marines and sailors, 50 Italians, 50 Frenchmen, 90 Germans and 25 Japanese. Their heavy weapons comprised one Colt and one Nordenfeldt machine gun, and an obsolete Italian 1-pounder cannon.

Events took a turn for the worse when the Japanese Chancellor was hacked to death by Chinese soldiers outside the Legation area on 11 June. On the 19th, the foreigners were told to leave Peking within 24 hours, but the diplomats decided that the long journey through China

would be too dangerous, and that it was safer to sit tight and wait until they could be rescued by a relief force. The German Chancellor was sent to the Foreign Office to state this view, but he too was killed by soldiers.

The Legation Quarter was now under siege, both by Boxers and by regular Chinese troops. Barricades were hastily constructed to protect the foreign quarter, although some national legation buildings were too far away to be defended and were abandoned. These defenses originally consisted of a few handcarts across access roads, but more secure obstacles were soon built from sandbags, timber, rubble and earth. The southern perimeter was the Tartar wall, a high barrier wider than a highway, with German and US troops stationed on top in sand-bagged bunkers along one side, and the Chinese along the other. There were now some 3000 civilians within the barricades, including missionaries, traders, diplomats and Chinese who had converted to Christianity. More by luck than foresight, the Legation quarter had ample stocks of grain and tinned food, while over 150 horses provided a source of meat. Water was supplied from numerous wells, and the defenders estimated that they had over 12 weeks worth of supplies.

Chinese soldiers and Boxer fanatics carried out numerous attacks, attempting to push into the quarter from various directions. A series of brisk actions took place, with soldiers and armed civilians repelling the assaults one by one. A weak spot in the defense was the open gardens at Fu in the northeast, the sector allocated to the Japanese. Their 25 riflemen, supported by over 30 civilian volunteers, stopped repeated attacks by the Chinese with deadly, accurate rifle-fire, although by the end of the siege every Japanese soldier was hit and wounded at least once.

When these attacks failed, the Chinese set fire to a number of buildings in the hope that the flames would spread and destroy Legation buildings. The defenders would have to drive the Chinese back before extinguishing the flames, and for his actions on one of these sorties Captain Lewis Halliday of the Royal Marines was awarded the Victoria Cross. Another dangerous moment was on 1 July, when the Chinese managed to eject the Germans and Americans from the Tartar wall – a success which threatened the whole of the defense. Captain Myers of the US Marine Corps, with a mixed force of just over 50 British and American Marines, and Russians, launched a hasty counterattack which drove the Chinese off the wall after some bitter fighting.

While all this was going on, the western nations were organizing a relief expedition. Over 2000 troops had already tried to get to Peking from Tientsin, but had been stopped by the Boxers and had ended up fighting for their own lives. By 20 June, however, the allied forces had assembled an army of over 20,000 men, which set off on the long trek to Peking. The biggest single contingent was some 8000

ABOVE: The Tartar wall was both a valuable adjunct to the defenses, and a formidable obstacle to the relief force.

RIGHT: This corner of the British Legation, pictured after the siege, shows the scars and damage of a fierce battle.

LEFT: *General Chaffee enters Peking in command of the American contingent of the relief expedition.*

BELOW LEFT: *British troops climb on to one of the city walls. This photograph may have been taken after the fighting had stopped.*

Japanese but there were also large numbers of Russian, British, American and French troops. They had to fight their way forward, but by about 13 August they were within striking distance of the walled city. The plan was for each national contingent to attack simultaneously from a different direction, but the Russians had seen what they thought was a lightly guarded gate and attacked early. They soon ran into trouble and suffered heavy casualties in forcing the wall.

The Chinese realized that their siege must soon come to an end one way or another, and launched some of the most violent and desperate attacks yet seen. In the meantime, the other national contingents in the relief force were hastily sent forward, the Americans having to scale the walls with no help from any gates. The British under General Gaselee used their artillery to blast through the walls into the Chinese City, and soon came to the Tartar Wall. They could hear fighting and could see flags still fly-ing above the Legations – all they had to do now was get over the wall. As they looked, a figure was seen waving signal flags from the roof of one of the buildings. "Come in by the sewer" was the message. So at 1430 hours on 13 August 1900, the first troops of the relieving force cut through rusty iron gratings and waded through black stinking mud to greet the delighted defenders. The leading soldiers were actually Indians in British service, the first regiment being Rajputs, followed by the Sikhs and the Royal Welch Fusiliers. After 55 days, the siege of the Legations was over.

Sixty-six westerners had died and 150 were wounded, but there is no clear record of Chinese casualties. The Dowager Empress was forced to flee as the allied troops took control of Peking, eventually imposing a harsh peace which involved reparations and increased interference in China's affairs. The Boxer rebellion had been crushed, but the cause of Chinese nationalism would flicker on.

BELOW: A multi-national group of officers from the relief force pose for the photographer after the rebellion has been crushed.

LEFT: *Like most rebellions, bloody reprisals followed the end of the fighting. Here, a Boxer is being publicly executed.*

125

Verdun

1916

". . . the French General Staff would be compelled to throw in every man they have. If they do so the forces of France will bleed to death . . ."

ERICH VON FALKENHAYN

THE WESTERN FRONT in World War I saw some of the bloodiest and most gruesome battles of attrition in history, but perhaps the worst of all in terms of the suffering of the participants was that of Verdun. For nearly 10 months in 1916 the French and German armies tore at each other in a sector only 18 miles wide by 5 miles deep, one within which nearly 270,000 men died and almost 700,000 were wounded. By the end of the battle no strategic gains had been achieved; there were no great breakthroughs and no sweeping maneuvers. Instead, the horror of this battle left such an impression on the minds of the participants that it affected their conduct during the remaining years of this war, and their preparation for the next.

BELOW: *Erich von Falkenhayn was the driving force behind the German plan to attack at Verdun.*

The decision to attack toward the fortress town of Verdun was taken in late December 1915 by the German Commander in Chief, Erich von Falkenhayn. Frustrated by the failure of the Schlieffen plan in 1914 and the subsequent stalemate, he was anxious to put France out of the war before British and Russian strength grew enough to overwhelm Germany. His plan was to attack in a place that the French would have to defend, and where his artillery could grind down the French Army, or as he put it, "bleed them white." He realized that Verdun had an almost mystical symbolism to the French military mind after the war of 1870, and it had been a lynchpin in the Allied lines when the German advance of 1914 was finally stopped. Here was a place that the French High Command could never surrender – here was an ideal place to draw their army in to be slaughtered.

The German formation chosen to lead the attack was the Fifth Army, led by the royal heir himself, the youthful Crown Prince. He was told to attack toward Verdun, but it appears that Falkenhayn's true intentions were never made clear. The Crown Prince assumed that Verdun was a genuine objective, so he planned on attacking on both banks of the River Meuse, pinching out the bulging salient formed by French forces around the town. Falkenhayn overruled his scheme, insisting instead on a much narrower frontage on the right (east) bank only. He also limited the Prince's forces to nine divisions, anxious to keep large reserves back to counter a probable British attack in the spring.

From December to February the Germans prepared for their offensive. Extra railway spurs were built to allow the constant flow of men and materiel to the front, while the greatest concentration of artillery yet seen was put in motion. The most impressive heavy guns were the massive short-barreled mortars which fired one-ton shells of 42cm diameter, and which would be used to shatter the thick concrete of the French fortifications. There were also heavy guns of 38cm, 30.5cm and 21cm caliber, as well as a host of smaller types adding up to 1200 guns in total. Their fire would be concentrated on an eight-mile front.

The build-up was carefully concealed from French spies and aerial reconnaissance, with the guns and their ammunition dumps only brought forward at night, then carefully camouflaged with nets and painted canvas screens. The huge numbers of troops assembling for the assault were also hidden from prying eyes, and many were held in huge underground galleries dug nearly 1000 yards behind the front. This camouflage combined with a number of diversions and deceptions was remarkably effective in fooling the French High Command, although the troops nearer the front line had more of an inkling of what was about to hit them.

Marshal Joseph Joffre was the French Commander in Chief, a man whose main military virtue was an unshakeable calm and self-confidence. As the Germans prepared for their attack, his main concern was planning the Allied offensive scheduled for that year. Ignoring warnings from the Verdun sector, he believed that the risk of a major German attack was exaggerated. General Herr, the Governor of Verdun was worried by the state of his defenses, but was told by Joffre not to concern himself. In Herr's sector the front curved out in a 15-mile bulge, with the city itself at the center. Numerous forts and gun emplacements lay between the city and the front, although the rolling hilly countryside on the right bank of the Meuse gave good cover for an enemy to march past them. There were two large fortifications which formed important bastions in the defense. The largest, Douaumont, loomed above the countryside, a great concrete block on a hilltop some 1200 feet above sea level. Over 400 yards across and with a plan shaped like a giant flattened "M," it had a roof more than eight feet thick and had galleries sunk more than three stories underground. Numerous heavy guns had been emplaced in steel turrets which could be retracted below ground level if under heavy fire. Unfortunately the French doctrine of "offensive spirit" had ensured that almost all of the guns on this and other fortresses had been removed to be used in a more mobile role. The second largest fort in the area was at Vaux, which was a smaller

ABOVE: *The German Crown Prince led the Fifth Army, the formation that spearheaded the assault.*

LEFT: *Heavy artillery was used in unprecedented numbers to smash the French trenches and fortifications.*

ABOVE: These French soldiers are supposedly near Fort Douaumont, although their gun is a captured German MG08.

BELOW: In the initial days the German attack was so overwhelming that thousands of Frenchmen were taken prisoner.

the French in a fearsome hurricane of a bombardment. Trenches and dugouts were blasted, collapsing into muddy craters as the French front line disintegrated into a chaotic mess. Long range guns searched out railway junctions, concentration areas, artillery batteries and supply dumps, with gas shells mixed in with the high explosive. At times the shelling would stop, causing the survivors to rush out and man what was left of their trenches, helping the observers identify the targets that needed more treatment. The French guns were almost completely silenced by this firestorm; outnumbered and blinded, their only response was to fire sporadically at predetermined points.

At 1600 hours the first German soldiers advanced, hoping to bypass any remaining pockets of resistance. Small groups of skirmishers dashed forward, making use of available cover as they came. The German corps commanders' decision to use these scouting parties along most of the front was perhaps overcautious, though, and a valuable opportunity to smother the dazed enemy was missed. The only corps not to do this was von Zwehl's VII Reserve Corps, where assault groups followed immediately after the skirmishers. The opening day also saw the first use of a uniquely terrifying infantry weapon – the flamethrower. At first, they were deadly in wiping out any positions that still held, but French marksmen would soon discover the vulnerability of their operators with their tanks of inflammable fuel.

For the next two days the Germans pressed forward, fighting through a landscape that they thought had been swept clean of all enemy. But like the British would do a few months later,

version of Douaumont and similarly denuded of guns. The trench lines around these positions were also poorly constructed, although some efforts were being made to improve them before the attack came.

Throughout January the preparations continued, with 12 February being the chosen date for the offensive. On the day, thick snow and mist obscured visibility and prevented the German artillery observers from seeing their targets, so the attack was postponed. This state of affairs continued for over a week, and it was not until 0700 hours on the 20th that the first shells were fired. Heavy projectiles rained down on

they were discovering that the artillery barrage had not been as lethal as it looked. Little groups of men were surfacing from the churned trenches, shooting at the advancing troops and even launching tiny local counterattacks. Virtually all French communications with the rear had been cut, so the conduct of the defense devolved on the junior officers, NCO's and soldiers in the front line. Without leadership, without supplies and without artillery support they fought on. Each counterattack would cost more of their lives, but the sum effect was a slowing and bogging down of the German attack.

The first crisis for the defense came on the 24th, when much of the French line finally gave way. In a remarkable coup, a tiny party of Brandenburgers reached Fort Douaumont to find it virtually unguarded, with only a few men manning the remaining artillery piece. Entering the fort through a gunport they padded around like cat burglars until they captured the shocked and unprepared garrison. By the end of the day the way to Verdun appeared open, although by now the Germans were too battered and exhausted to take much advantage of it.

That night Joffre's Chief of Staff, General de Castelnau, arrived in Verdun to see the situation for himself. Realizing the depth of the crisis, he ordered the French Second Army forward from the reserve, giving its commander General Pétain overall control of the Verdun defenses. Before Pétain arrived, de Castelnau surveyed the deteriorating position, and the next day made the single most important decision of the battle. Verdun would be defended at all costs. A more cautious man may have seen virtue in slowly retreating to the left bank of the Meuse, avoiding the ferocious shelling while inflicting large numbers of casualties on the Germans, but de Castlenau would have nothing of it. A fiery, aggressive man who was by instinct a fighter, he believed firmly in the symbolic meaning of Verdun for the French people, and that retreat was out of the question. With this decision he set the seal on the pattern of the battle, one which would remain constant for the next 10 months.

The man he had selected to lead the defense was a cold, aloof figure who nevertheless cared deeply about the fate of his soldiers. One of the most admired and respected men in the army, Henri Philippe Pétain did not subscribe to the almost mythical belief in the offensive spirit that was the docrine of most of his contemporaries. Instead, he had realized earlier than most

ABOVE: *The railroad was used to bring in reinforcements from all over France, although they had to make their way up a single, narrow shell-torn road to reach the front.*

LEFT: *The calm competence and iron will of Pétain helped stabilize the French front line and blunt the German attack.*

FAR RIGHT: The initial German attack was on the right bank of the Meuse only. It was only after two weeks of fighting that Fifth Army was allowed to widen the attack to the left bank.

BOTTOM RIGHT: German soldiers pose in front of one of the destroyed guns in Fort Vaux.

BELOW: Many French colonial regiments fought in the freezing wet mud of Verdun.

the effectiveness of machine guns, wire and artillery in stopping unprotected infantry. His methodical, scientific approach to war was in stark contrast to the amateur aggressiveness of other French officers, and his care in planning had won the thankful appreciation of his men, who felt that their commander would always do what he would to make their lives easier. The irony of Verdun was that the battle he was about to fight was one where the common soldier could suffer unbelievable deprivation and misery, enduring months of danger and exhaustion. If Pétain had been given a free hand he probably would have selected the withdrawal option, but de Castlenau had already made that decision for him.

News of Pétain's arrival immediately boosted French morale, although for the first week he had to command from his sick-bed. One of his early actions was to reorganize his artillery so that the individual batteries cooperated in massive co-ordinated fire missions; and within a few days his guns had become almost as effective as those of the Germans in harassing supply routes and breaking up attacks. His next priority was the French supply system, which had almost completely broken

down. Road and rail links had been cut by the shelling, and the only remaining supply route was a single road into Verdun with a narrow gauge light railroad alongside. Along this fragile artery would have to travel every shell, bullet, scrap of food, and drop of water needed by the 500,000 men in the Verdun salient. They would also have to share the road with the reinforcements moving to the front and the few overworked ambulances bringing the wounded soldiers back.

Pétain's supply officer immediately set about scrounging every truck, car and wagon he could find, and his herculean efforts produced more than 4000 vehicles. A complex system of traffic control was organized, whereby trucks would pass up this road every few seconds, night and day, even when under heavy shelling. If a vehicle was hit or broken down it was just shoved aside and left – nothing must hinder the traffic. Thousands of colonial and territorial troops were used to maintain this link, using tons of gravel and rubble to fill shell holes and shore up areas of collapsing track. For months this single road would be the sole lifeline for the defense of Verdun, earning it the later epithet of "Voie Sacrée" or "Sacred Road."

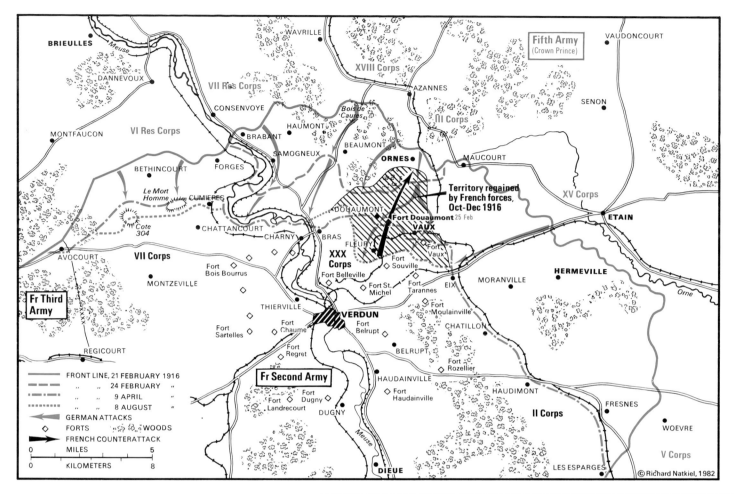

The German attack had stalled, so on 3 March the Crown Prince was given four more divisions to expand his offensive to the west bank of the Meuse. This time the French were expecting him, although it took three days of bitter fighting around the high ground of Le Mort Homme before the German advance was stopped. After this attack the character of the battle changed. Gone was any hope of movement and rapid advances, all that was left was bloody, grinding attrition.

The German attack had faltered, but Falkenhayn still pressed his strategy of "bleeding the French dry." Unfortunately, his men were dying in almost as great a number as their enemy. It was hard to see who was winning, but it was certain that both sides were doing a lot of bleeding. This battle had taken on a life of its own, with all thoughts of strategic gain or benefit ignored. Both sides were simply feeding the mincing machine. There was no real front line, just a nightmarish moonscape of mud and shell craters, with only the occasional section of trench still intact. Bodies lay everywhere in various stages of decomposition: it was later calculated that more dead lay in each acre of ground than in any other battle of modern times. Wherever a man lay or dug there would

ABOVE: A German soldier takes cover in a recently captured French trench.

BELOW: Eventually the tide turned. Now it was German soldiers who were being marched off into captivity.

French medical services were totally inadequate for the number and type of casualties inflicted. If a man was hit, the first step was to get carried back to the Clearing Station, but often even this hurdle could not be overcome. Exhaustion and strain had created a spiritual numbness among many men, and a soldier who was wounded was often left lying and ignored. Should a stretcher party pick him up he then had to endure the bumpy slithering journey over the mud, under constant bombardment. The aid post itself would be a nightmare, with men sometimes waiting days for treatment. Inadequate drugs, insufficient doctors and sheer weight of numbers all added to the chaos. The surgeons could only spend time on those they thought could soon be returned to service, anyone who looked too badly injured to survive, or whose wounds were too complicated for immediate help, was normally left outside on stretchers in the mud. On one occasion such a Clearing Station was visited by an Inspector-General, whose one contribution was to suggest that flower tubs be planted to raise morale. The comments of the Surgeons and their charges were not recorded.

By mid-April, Joffre was unhappy with Pétain's careful defensive strategy. He wanted a glorious offensive, and in his protegé General Nivelle he thought he had just the man. On 19 April, Pétain was promoted upstairs to command the army group in a thinly-disguised removal, while the dynamic, aggressive and supremely self-confident Nivelle was given command of the Verdun sector. Not only would the French soldiers have to endure the hell of the front line, they would now be expected to launch a futile series of attacks as well.

Through May and June the Germans were also still trying to move forward, and on 2nd June they managed to get an assault group into the fort at Vaux. For five days a vicious battle took place in the corridors and galleries of the underground complex, with men shooting and throwing grenades at each other from a few feet away. Eventually the French surrendered, although they had caused over 2600 casualties among the attackers. Overall though, the German pressure was receding and Falkenhayn was showing the vacillation and indecision that he already had a reputation for. He refused to reinforce the German assault but at the same time was equally unwilling to stop the battle, instead claiming that the French were near collapse. They were near collapse – but then so were the Germans.

be remnants of flesh or complete corpses, even floating in the muddy puddles that were the only source of drinking water for many. Conditions on both sides were appalling, but the French soldier probably suffered more due to the notorious inefficiency of his supply and medical services. Dysentry, that scourge of medieval warfare, was common, and most men's uniforms were infested with lice. Food was scarce, having to be brought forward by volunteer couriers who had to carry the bread and wine in makeshift bags or bundles tied to their person. German gunners knew the likely routes used, so these men had to run a regular gauntlet of shells, all too often being killed.

A last attack was launched on 23 June, and this one almost achieved a startling victory. German chemists had developed Phosgene, a new and deadly gas that could penetrate the respirators of the time. This new horror came close to finally breaking the French resistance, killing infantrymen and gun crews alike in a silent green choking cloud, and giving the Germans a breakthrough which got them to within two miles of Verdun. But four months of constant fighting had worn the attackers down too, and this final German offensive petered out around 15 July.

In the meantime, the British push on the Somme had started, although they had suffered their own disaster when over 60,000 of Kitchener's New Army had fallen in one devastating day. Nevertheless the German High Command now had to concern themselves both with this threat and that from Russia – and the hemorrhage of Verdun had to be stopped. The failure of his grand scheme finished Falkenhayn, his inevitable resignation being gratefully accepted. The Germans now dug themselves into a purely defensive posture while the determined French pushed back at them, regaining territory in a slow and painful process which only ended on 15 December.

ABOVE: This photograph purports to be of actual combat between advance patrols. Getting such a clear view of his target was a comparatively rare event for a rifleman on the Western front.

LEFT: French troops among the battered ruins of Fort Vaux.

ABOVE: Various designs of trench mortar were often used to drop bombs into opposing positions.

Who had won? Certainly not the common soldier. Over 165,000 Frenchmen were dead and 337,000 wounded, while the Germans had lost over 100,000 dead and 340,000 wounded. The psychological effects were also important. The Germans would now stay on the defensive on the Western Front until their desperate last throw in 1918, while the effects on the French Army would lead to the disastrous collapse and mutinies of 1917. From the summer of 1916, the British would take the lead on the Western Front.

The echoes of Verdun would also linger long after the war, with the story assuming almost religious overtones among the French military. The horrors and the casualties of the trenches, combined with the experience of defending Fort Vaux were a major influence on the creation of the Maginot line in the 1930s, and on French attitudes in 1940. The Germans took another lesson. Among the staff of the Fifth Army was a young Heinz Guderian, whose concept of mobile armored warfare produced the 1940 Blitzkrieg – an effort to avoid another ghastly slaughter like that of Verdun.

RIGHT: Many small villages around Verdun were turned into strongpoints and saw scenes of bitter fighting.

Okinawa

1945

"It is going to be really tough, there are 65-70,000 fighting Japanese holed up in the south end of the island. I see no way to get them out except to blast them out yard by yard."

MAJOR GENERAL JOHN R. HODGES

IN OCTOBER 1944, the US Joint Chiefs of Staff made several important decisions that defined how the war against Japan would proceed through early 1945. General MacArthur was to begin the liberation of the Philippines almost immediately, while Admiral Nimitz would invade Iwo Jima the following February. If all went according to plan, the invasion of Okinawa would begin soon after.

Okinawa is the largest island in the Ryukyus group, a rugged and mountainous place some 75 miles long but only 7-10 miles wide. At that time it had a population of nearly 450,000, which was ethnically related to the Japanese but with ancient cultures and languages of its own. Their island had been part of the Japanese empire since 1879, and many Okinawans were serving in the Japanese forces and in a poorly-armed "Home Guard." Situated within 360 miles of the southern Japanese mainland, Okinawa's large natural harbors and good-sized airfields would provide an ideal springboard for the final invasion of Japan. Ships and aircraft operating from here would also cut Japan's supply routes to Formosa and East China. Another less tangible reason for invading was that Okinawa would be the first "Japanese" territory taken by the Americans, and so its loss would be a huge psychological blow.

The American force chosen to carry out the landings on Okinawa was Task Force 51 (TF51). Led by Vice-Admiral Richmond "Kelly" Turner, TF51's 1500 warships, supply vessels and amphibious craft would transport and support the 180,000 men of Tenth Army, a joint Marines/Army formation commanded by Lieutenant General Simon Bolivar Buckner Jnr. His army would comprise two corps with six combat-experienced divisions; Major General Roy Geiger's III Amphibious Corps with the 1st and 6th Marine Divisions, and Major General John Hodges XXIV Army Corps with the 7th and 96th Infantry Divisions. The 27th Infantry

Division would be held in reserve while the 77th Infantry Division would be used to attack the smaller islands immediately to the west of Okinawa. Buckner would also have the use of the 2nd Marine Division as a diversion force, although it would not be landed. Codenamed Operation "Iceberg" and scheduled to take place on 1 April 1945, the landing of the Tenth Army would be the largest such operation undertaken in the Pacific war, and one that would rival D-Day in scale.

The Okinawa defenses were the responsibility of the Thirty-second Army under Lieutenant General Mitsuru Ushijima, which was a force of around 77,000 men, with varying degrees of combat experience. He had two full infantry divisions, the 62nd and the 24th, with the 44th Independent Mixed Brigade as a separate command. There were also some 20,000 Okinawans in their Home Guard force. His army was well equipped by Japanese standards, with over 230 artillery pieces and

BELOW: *Amphibious landings in the Pacific used vast amonts of supporting firepower. Here the battleship* New Mexico *blasts 16in shells toward suspected Japanese positions on Okinawa.*

finement for this operation would be the first deliberate large scale use of kamikaze suicide pilots.

March 1945 saw a series of air attacks from American aircraft carriers in an attempt to neutralize Japanese air power. Light bombers struck at airfields in Japan, on Formosa, on Okinawa itself, and on other islands within range. The British carrier group, Task Force 57, also took part in these strikes. The Japanese hit back, severely damaging a number of American ships, including the carrier USS *Franklin*, which limped back to New York after an epic battle with the fires and destruction caused by multiple bomb hits. On 24 March, the first landings of the campaign were made, when the 77th Infantry Division assaulted the Kerama group, a small cluster of islands 15 miles to the west of Okinawa. The 77th took three days to gain control of the Keramas, but achieved an unexpected bonus when they cap-

ABOVE: Knowledge of the effectiveness of the US Navy's shore bombardment caused Ushijima to deploy his troops inland, away from the beaches.

more than the usual number of mortars, anti-aircraft guns, anti-tank guns and machine guns. Even so, by this stage in the war the Imperial Army was totally outclassed in terms of weaponry by the Americans, whose units had more and better artillery, armor and firepower. The Americans could also take advantage of massive aerial superiority, supplemented in an amphibious landing by naval gunfire support. As well as having a preponderance of equipment, the Americans had learned from their early disasters and were now highly skilled fighters, able to launch complex operations in the most inhospitable terrains.

Ushijima's mission was to hold back an American attack as long as possible, buying precious time for his homeland. He and his men were to make the enemy pay dearly for every foot of ground, causing heavy casualties and forcing them to commit massive resources which could be used elsewhere. There would be no withdrawal from Okinawa, the Japanese soldiers were expected to fight and die where they stood. In the months before the invasion, Ushijima had pleaded for reinforcements, extra weapons and more supplies, but his superiors could spare very little. He would have to rely on what he had – and the renowned fighting spirit, courage and refusal to surrender that characterized the Japanese Army. One bright spot was that he would have the help of nearly 3600 aircraft which were stationed within range of Okinawa. The plan was to launch massive attacks on the ships supporting any landing. A new re-

RIGHT: Lieutenant General Simon Bolivar Buckner (on the right) was in command of Tenth Army. He was killed by a Japanese shell just as the battle was drawing to a close.

tured hundreds of small motor boats, packed with explosives and intended for use in suicide attacks on an invasion fleet.

In the meantime Turner's battleships and cruisers had moved into range behind their covering screen of minesweepers, and began a week-long bombardment of the island's defenses. On the morning of 1 April, the leading elements of four US divisions came ashore near Hagushi Bay, toward the southwest of the island. The 6th Marine Division was at the north of the beachead, south of which were the

1st Marine Division, the 7th Infantry Division and the 96th Infantry Division. At the same time the 2nd Marine Division dragged their coattails past the west side of the island, drawing numerous Japanese aircraft away from the real landing site. On the actual assault beaches, the troops were stunned to find virtually no resistance, with the Japanese limiting themselves to occasional small pockets of resistance and sporadic shelling. By the end of that day, nearly 60,000 men were ashore in a textbook landing.

Ushijima had realized that Turner's naval firepower would be too powerful for any coastal defenses to resist and had decided to make his stand elsewhere. Going against the shrill outpourings from his distant superiors about holding every inch of sacred soil, he abandoned the flat central plain and its airfields, and dug his troops into the mountainous jungle terrain in the south tip of the island. His strategy was to remain on the defensive, giving ground slowly while causing as many casualties as possible. It was a much more sophisticated defensive strategy than that normally employed by the Japanese, and one that would give the Americans uniquely difficult problems.

Within a few days the invaders had secured the central part of the island. The marine divisions of III Amphibious Corps were sweeping northward into the Motubu peninsula, while the two divisions of XXIV Army Corps forced their way south. On 6 April, the army came to Ushijima's first defense line, manned by his 62nd Division, and Hodge's 7th Division engaged it in a bitter two-day fight for prominent high ground known as the Pinnacle. The marines in the north had also met stiffer opposition, and were now having to fight their way forward more slowly.

That day also saw the navy's first taste of what was to become a common experience, when some 700 aircraft bombed and strafed the transports and warships clustered around the island. Over 300 of these machines were flown by kamikaze suicide pilots, taking part in the first massed "kikusi" attack by this uniquely Japanese weapon. Being the target of such an attack was a terrifying experience, where one could only watch the tiny fighter boring inward through the flak, knowing that nothing short of a direct hit would stop it. Those aircraft that hit their targets would cause immense damage when they exploded, and by the end of that day three destroyers were sunk, along with two ammunition ships and a tank-landing vessel. Ten more ships were seriously damaged. This first kikusi attack set the pattern for the next three months, where the United States Navy would suffer more losses than in any other battle of the war.

Suicide missions were not confined to the airmen, and a bizarre plan was hatched which

BELOW: Veterans of many amphibious assaults, these marines were amazed to find no resistance as they landed on the beaches.

ABOVE: Landing craft and tracked "Buffalo" assault transports ply back and forward between the fleet and the beach.

LEFT: Two weeks after the first landings, and wheeled support vehicles are still being brought ashore. They are fueled once on the beach to reduce the fire risk when afloat. Note the pile of discarded fuel drums.

ABOVE: *The deck elevator of USS Sangborn lies twisted and buckled the day after a kamikaze strike on 4 May.*

RIGHT: *British carriers with their armored decks were better able to withstand such attacks, although the penalty was reduced hangar space.*

FAR RIGHT: The bitter nature of the fighting saw many "non-battle" and psychiatric casualties. This man has just witnessed the death of his buddy.

BELOW FAR RIGHT: Almost every yard of the island had to be fought for in a close-range, bloody struggle.

BELOW: The battleship Yamato *blows up after being attacked by US Navy aircraft.*

involved the few remaining powerful surface units of the Imperial Japanese Navy. The battleship *Yamato* was still one of the most powerful warships in the world, although the lack of fuel and a trained crew were a hindrance to her effectiveness. In a spectacularly extravagant gesture she was sent, with two cruisers as escort but with no air cover, on a one-way mission to wreak what damage she could on the American invasion fleet before beaching herself on the island as a sort of steel pillbox. The mission was a humiliating failure, with the Japanese ships being spotted by an American submarine almost as soon as they set out from Kure, and being pounded beneath the waves the next day by 300 US aircraft.

In the north of the island, the marines continued to snuff out resistance, until the last Japanese units were left fighting a guerrilla-style action from the Yae Take hills, where they would hold out until 20 April. In the south, Hodges launched his two divisions against the main Japanese line of resistance based around the small town of Shuri. It was here that the full scope of the Japanese preparations first became apparent. Machine-gun posts, mortars

and anti-tank guns were all skillfully sited and camouflaged, many in underground bunkers and caves. Firing positions were often situated on reverse slopes, where they could not be identified by artillery spotters and where they could get clear shots at the Americans as they came over the crests. Interlocking arcs had been carefully calculated so that each position was supported by others, forming a deadly web of firelanes and target zones.

Progress against this was a painfully slow, nerve-racking crawl. The Japanese bunkers went deep underground and many were protected by thick concrete, so that most of their occupants remained unharmed by even the most prolonged and heavy shelling or bombing. When the Americans inched their way forward, shooting would erupt from what appeared to be tiny holes in the hillside, often from previously unseen positions. They had to be taken out one by one, with satchel charges, grenades or tank shells pumped into their firing slits. Many such caves were just blown in, leaving the occupants entombed under the earth and rubble. The Japanese artillery would also rain down short sharp bombardments which made it difficult for the Americans to locate the well-camouflaged guns.

This deadly network was further enhanced by the refusal of the Japanese fighting man to surrender, and his determination to sell his life as dearly as possible. Men would make sudden counterattacks, sometimes running toward American tanks with satchel charges clutched in their arms, to be detonated once close to their target. Others would resist shells, bullets, incendiary phosphorous and bombs, shooting as long as their ammunition lasted. Casualties were high on both sides, but the sheer weight of American firepower was taking its toll. Japanese soldiers and Okinawan auxiliaries were being blasted, burned and shredded by the hundred, with nearly 10 dying for every American casualty.

By 12 April, the attacks of both the 7th and 96th Infantry Divisions had stalled, with the 7th Division being held by a particularly well-prepared position at Kakazu Hill. It was at this time that the prejudices and blindness of the Japanese High Command made themself felt. Querulous messages reminded Ushijima that the spirit of the Japanese fighting man was greatly superior to that of the decadent Americans – and insisted that he recapture the abandoned airfields. Ushijima could not resist this pressure from above, especially as his

Chief of Staff and many of his officers agreed with the sentiment. So on the night of the 12th, the Japanese came out of their bunkers and their caves in a futile attempt to push back the invaders. Although surprise gave them some initial successes, they were eventually blown apart by American firepower, and the attacks fizzled out with nothing gained.

Both sides spent the next few days licking their wounds, with the Americans preparing to renew their attacks. On 16 April, the 77th Division, which had been consolidating its hold on the Kerama Islands, was sent to land on Ie Shima, another island just offshore from the Motobu peninsula. It was here that the Americans first came up against determined resistance from the Okinawan civilians, 5000 of whom fought alongside their Japanese rulers. Some had rifles, but many were only armed with wooden spears. After a short but bloody campaign, the island was secured by the 21st.

Vice-Admiral Turner was by now complaining of the slow progress made by the Army. His ships were being battered and sunk every day, while Hodges' men seemed to have been almost immobile for nearly two weeks. Typical

of the tensions that arise between the land and sea components of an amphibious operation, Turners' complaints did not go down well with the men face-to-face with the Japanese in the mud and rain of the monsoon.

By 19 April, the troops were ready to attack again, even though many of the front line units were showing signs of overwhelming combat fatigue. Buckner had now given Hodges his single reserve division, and the 27th Infantry entered the line alongside the tired and battered 7th and 96th. Artillery, naval gunfire and tactical air power were all used in greater strength than before, and over 19,000 shells were fired in one 40 minute spasm. The Americans also brought forward Sherman tanks equipped with flamethrowers, which could pour great jets of burning fuel into trenches, bunkers and caves. Savage fighting took place over the next few days, until the Japanese withdrew from the Kakazu ridge on the 24th.

This was no breakthrough, however, as Ushijima's men pulled back in good order to their next line of defenses, a few miles closer to Shuri. So far his strategy was working better than anyone expected. On the 25th the Americans launched their attack on this new position, going through the same bloody and frustrating process of having to destroy each bunker one at a time. Faced with a seemingly unending series of frontal attacks, some American officers argued for putting a marine division ashore behind the Japanese lines, but Buckner set himself firmly against this, reason-

BELOW: While obsolescent as an anti-tank weapon, the US M3A1 37mm AT gun was effective against enemy pillboxes.

ing that the landing force would be too small and would just get itself into serious trouble.

Coincidentally, just as the amphibious landing idea was rejected, Ushijimi had been forced to move his 24th Division, which had been guarding his southern coastline, up into the line to supplement the badly reduced 62nd Division. The Americans also reinforced their front, with the 1st Marine Division temporarily coming under Hodges' control. They replaced the battle-weary 27th Infantry, while the 77th were brought up to relieve the 96th.

Early May saw another period of stalemate, which was broken in a manner which totally surprised the Americans. Lieutenant General Isamo Cho, Ushijima's Chief of Staff and a fiery, aggressive soldier in the best traditions of the Imperial Army, had continually pressed for a counterattack, and in the first week of May, his commander finally agreed. A careful plan was constructed where the comparatively fresh 24th Division was to punch through the American lines with 15,000 men while small groups would make amphibious landings on the east and west coasts in an effort to disrupt supply lines and artillery. The carefully husbanded Japanese artillery would join in with the most powerful barrage they had yet fired, and the few remaining Japanese light tanks would also be used in this all-out assault. On 4 May after a 30-minute bombardment, Ushijima's men advanced toward the American lines, with the exhortation to "kill one American devil for every Japanese" ringing in their ears.

Surprise was almost complete, with the lead troops moving through their own barrage into the front lines of the 7th Infantry Division. The stunned Americans took something of a battering from the shelling, not having the advantage of deep shelters and bunkers. Some early gains were made, but both the 7th and 77th Divisions recovered quickly, and the Japanese were soon being chopped down by superior American firepower. After two days and 5000 dead, the attack was called off. All the Japanese tanks were destroyed and many of the guns had been located and attacked; the defenses were now significantly weaker, and the Japanese had gained nothing.

Within a few days, both American corps were in the line. Buckner's Tenth Army headquarters was now in overall command of the assault, although the hard pressed navy were still complaining of the slow speed of advance. On the 9th the attack was renewed. The fighting was just as hard as before, with long

bitter battles being fought over any high ground, such as the 6th Marines epic 10-day struggle for the feature known as Sugar Loaf Hill. On the 14th, the 96th Infantry gained a toehold on the formidable position known as Conical Hill, which finally broke open the Japanese line on the right flank. The Thirty-second Army's fighting strength was now only a third of what it had been before the invasion, and their whole Shuri position was now seriously threatened.

Ushijima's response was as effective as it was totally unexpected. In the last week of May his units started to pull back behind Shuri in a superbly-executed withdrawal, which was protected from American airpower by the atrocious weather. Instead of their enemy staying put to be shattered by devastating firepower, the Americans were dismayed to discover that he was now occupying newly dug positions centered on the Yaeju Dake escarpment. In the meantime, the 6th Marine Division had been pulled out of the line and landed on the Oruku peninsula to attack and destroy the Japanese naval base there.

June was spent in a series of small but violent attacks on the new Japanese positions, each one

ABOVE: *US forces quickly cleared the center and north of the island, but the Japanese made their main stand in the south.*

LEFT: *The story of USS* Franklin *became a national legend. Blasted by Japanese bombs and the resulting fires, she limped home to New York under her own power.*

capturing a few more yards of ground and killing a few hundred more defenders. After a while it became obvious that resistance was finally crumbling. The level of casualties had by now greatly weakened the defense, while exhaustion was finally wearing down the survivors. The Japanese were disintegrating, although it would take until 18 June before they finally fell apart as an organized unit. Even so, many isolated units fought on, while others took to guerrilla warfare alongside thousands of civilians. In the last days of the battle, Ushijima and Cho took the traditional way out for Japanese commanders who had been defeated, carrying out the ritual suicide of seppuku with their own swords. Buckner also paid the ultimate price for his victory, as on the 18th he was hit and killed by a fragment of coral flung up by an exploding shell.

The cost to the Japanese of the Okinawa battle had been enormous. Some 110,000 soldiers, sailors and airmen had died, while the total of only 7400 taken prisoner is a testament to their willingness to stand and die. Another grievous loss to the final defense of the homeland was more than 7000 aircraft which had been destroyed in the great battles around the island.

American casualties were not nearly so high, although they were still a fearsome amount for the survivors to absorb; 12,500 soldiers dead and 37,000 wounded, with 2900 marines dead and 13,700 wounded. The navy had lost 4900 men with 4800 wounded, while more than 34 major ships had gone to the bottom of the ocean with a further 368 heavily damaged. An indication of the strain of the fighting was the high total of 26,000 "non-battle" casualties, many suffering from battle fatigue and stress disorders. And what of the Okinawans? Precise figures are not known, but estimates of the dead have been as high as 160,000. Many were killed by aerial, naval and artillery bombardment, while thousands died alongside their Japanese masters in the caves and bunkers. Whatever the true number, it was an unbeliev-

BELOW: A US tank destroyer of the 77th Infantry Division fires into the enemy lines at Shuri.

able blow to the small population, who proportionally, suffered greater losses than any other nation during the war.

The lasting effect of Okinawa, however, was in the minds of the American politicians, soldiers and sailors who had to plan and execute the invasion of Japan. They had visions of a whole nation in arms, and were haunted by images of cave systems and bunkers, of fighting over the whole of Japan inch by inch, and of civilians charging machine guns, armed only with home-made spears. Estimates of the casualty roll were staggeringly high. In the end, the American commanders looked elsewhere for the answer. The terrible alternative to the invasion of Japan involved the deadly mushroom clouds over Hiroshima and Nagasaki, and ushered in a new era of warfare.

ABOVE: *Once organized resistance collapsed, isolated groups of Japanese began to give themselves up.*

Dien Bien Phu

1954

"We will take the French by the throat."

GENERAL VO NGUYEN GIAP

ONCE WORLD WAR II had ended, the French government attempted to regain their Far Eastern colonial possessions that had been overrun by the Japanese. In Vietnam and Laos they came up against strong resistance from Nationalist and Communist groups, who fought a long and bitter struggle for independence. By 1953 the strongest of these was known as the Viet Minh, led by a wily Nationalist-turned-Communist known as Ho Chi Minh. Having evolved from a few ragged peasants into a well trained, organized and equipped guerrilla army, they operated almost with impunity in the Vietnamese countryside. With

BELOW: Ho Chi Minh was the guiding light behind the Viet Minh, the guerrilla force that eventually threw the French out of Indo-China.

weapons supplied from Russia and China they were able to attack French outposts then melt into the thick forestation and jungle, where the clumsy French counterattacks would normally lose them.

The man given the difficult task of leading the French forces in Vietnam was General Henri Navarre, who even with an infusion of weapons and aircraft from the United States, had no illusions about eventual victory. His objective was to force a negotiated peace with honor, a necessary precondition of which was to achieve a military victory over the Viet Minh. The plan he evolved was to put a large French expedition in a position that would force the Viet Minh to attack them, and where the guerrillas would be destroyed by French firepower. The place he chose was a tiny village known as Dien Bien Phu.

Situated in the northwest corner of Vietnam, 10 miles from the Laotian border and 170 miles from Hanoi, Dien Bien Phu sits astride the crossroads of the main route into northern Laos and that from Burma and China. The village itself comprised 100 or so stilt huts around a disused Japanese airstrip in a deep round valley, with a cluster of low hills around it. Farther out were thickly forested high ridges and mountains, and to the south was a narrower valley and the road into Laos, giving the whole area a shape resembling a frying pan. Navarre's concept was that a powerful French force blocking these vital Viet Minh supply routes could not be ignored.

On 20 November 1953, American-built C-47 transport planes droned in the skies over Dien Bien Phu, dropping the 800 men of Colonel Marcel Bigeard's 6th Colonial Parachute Battalion. Operation Castor was under way. Within a few days the French had two airstrips functioning and were flying in more men and equipment and digging in around Dien Bien Phu. Their commander was Colonel Christian de

BELOW: *Colonel de Castries (driving) with the French defense minister and the Commander in Chief of the French in North Vietnam.*

RIGHT: *A French soldier on patrol to the east of Dien Bien Phu in January 1954, two months before the Viet Minh onslaught.*

BOTTOM: *These porters could push over 150lb of Viet Minh supplies on each one of their modified bicycles.*

ABOVE: *French paratroopers dropping from an ex-US C-47 transport to reinforce the garrison at Dien Bien Phu. The initial drop on Dien Bien Phu came as a complete surprise to Giap and Ho Chi Minh.*

trenches, machine-gun posts and bunkers. Most were on the shallow hills immediately surrounding the village, and in typically Gallic style they were identified by female names. The central bastion which also contained the airstrip and de Castries' HQ was known as "Claudine," while "Huguette," "Dominique," "Elaine" and "Francoise" were the main defensive positions. The next layer of outposts were "Anne-Marie" and "Beatrice," with "Gabrielle" in the far north. A second airstrip, six miles to the south, was protected by the strongpoint "Isabelle."

While the French were consolidating their positions, the Viet Minh leadership were considering their options. As the French had been so helpful as to stick their necks out in such a fashion, was this not a superb opportunity to deal them a devastating blow from which they would never recover? The military commander of the Viet Minh was a 44-year-old history teacher named Vo Nguyen Giap, the strategic genius behind their successes to date. He felt that sufficient superiority in numbers could be achieved to guarantee the defeat of the French enclave, so in December 1953, almost the whole military strength of the Viet Minh was put in motion.

Villages for hundreds of miles around were combed for porters; men, women and youths who would form a human supply train for Giap's army. Paths were cut through the thick jungle to avoid French aerial reconnaissance, along which some 20,000 people pushed ancient bicycles modified with bamboo crossbars from which 150 pounds of rice or ammunition were slung. From all over northern Vietnam Giap's combat units gathered. For this operation the unprecedented number of 50,000 troops would be used, operating in four divisions. Lightly equipped, wearing simple peasant clothing and carrying only their rifle, some ammunition and a handful of rice, these men filtered through the jungle, gathering in the hills overlooking the Dien Bien Phu position. Giap's strength would not only be in infantry however, and he set in motion the biggest gathering of heavy firepower his men had ever seen. Machine guns, mortars, anti-aircraft guns and artillery were manhandled across the rough terrain, the heavy guns being inched forward through the mud and undergrowth by mule and muscle power. Using cover and camouflage superbly, the Viet Minh managed to get their guns on to the high ground around the French defenses, where they would be able

Castries, and his force comprised some 15,000 men, including 12 combat battalions. The majority were Vietnamese and Colonial troops, but de Castries also had units of the Foreign Legion and the elite of the French "paras." His heavy fire support consisted of 28 105mm howitzers, while 10 American M24 light tanks gave him some form of armored mobility. Six Bearcat propeller-driven fighters sat at the end of the newly-created airstrip, while he could also call on French fighter, bomber and transport aircraft based around Hanoi.

The troops were deployed in nine mutually supporting strongpoints, each of roughly battalion strength and comprising a series of

to fire over open sights at targets they could see below them. By March, Giap would have 48 105mm howitzers and over 150 lighter guns, an artillery strength that would be a profound shock to the French.

As 1954 dawned, the French were realizing that they were about to be in for a rough time. Intelligence reports pointed to an unprecedented gathering of strength around Dien Bien Phu, although the secret of the heavy guns was never discovered. It was too late to back down though, they would never get the heavy equipment out, and anyway, it would be a devastating blow to French prestige in Indo-China. Notwithstanding scare reports in the international media and an attack of nerves among the politicians back home, the men on the ground were still cheerfully confident about their ability to win a famous victory.

In a remarkably precise snippet of intelligence, de Castries was informed that the attack would begin at 1700 hours on 13 March, and most Frenchmen felt relief that the battle would at last be under way. On the evening of the 13th, they sat in their foxholes, waiting for the supposedly ill-trained peasants to come charging toward them, but what they actually got was as terrifying as it was unexpected. A few minutes after 1700 hours, more than 200 artillery pieces opened fire, in a whirlwind of blast and shrapnel which ripped through the French positions. Not expecting such a bombardment,

ABOVE: *Vo Nguyen Giap (in the white suit) was the military genius behind the defeat of both the French, and over 20 years later, the Americans.*

LEFT: *Pathfinders watch as their comrades follow. French forces included large numbers of Vietnamese and Thai colonial troops.*

the defenders had not dug particularly deeply, and many of the bunkers lacked strong overhead protection. They had also chopped down much of the natural cover when building their positions, and their entrenchments were in clear view of the watchers in the hills. These were errors that they were now paying for in blood, and well over 500 men were killed in that first hour of shelling.

The guns stopped as the sun fell, which was the signal for the first massed infantry attack. The Viet Minh 312 Division with over 7000 fighting men swarmed on to Beatrice, wiping out the battalion of 700 men stationed there. Only 200 escaped. That night, the French artillery commander, Colonel Piroth, committed suicide with a hand grenade after the failure of his guns to have any noticeable effect on the enemy shelling.

The next three days followed a similar pattern – a hurricane bombardment followed by an overwhelming assault on one of the strongpoints. Gabrielle fell on the 14th, while Anne-Marie was taken on the 16th. In some cases the poorly-trained colonial troops abandoned their positions at the first sign of attack, although this has been exaggerated in some accounts. On the

16th, Marcel Bigeard and his battalion, who had been preparing to return to France, were dropped in to Dien Bien Phu for the second time. He found a scene of chaos and confusion, with de Castries almost resigned to disaster. With another paratroop officer, Colonel Pierre Langlais, Bigeard set about organizing the first French counterattack. Concentrating all the French artillery fire and calling in numerous air strikes, he pounded an enemy battalion which had penetrated to the east of Claudine, then followed up with an attack which virtually destroyed it. The success was a costly one, however, with most of Bigeard's best officers being lost in the assault.

Pressure from the Viet Minh continued, although the spectacular victories of the first few days were not repeated. They were now up against the main French points of resistance, and were suffering heavy casualties themselves. The shelling continued, however, and by the 27th, both the airstrips were no longer usable. Ammunition, food and medicine would now have to be dropped by parachute, a dangerous and inefficient way of supplying troops. The weather was often wet and cloudy, creating danger to the airmen from the surrounding

ABOVE: Paratroopers leaving their trenches to take part in one of the many counterattacks.

FAR LEFT: Once the power of Giap's artillery had been demonstrated, the French began to dig much deeper than before. The airfield is behind this trench, complete with wrecked transport aircraft.

151

ABOVE: As Viet Minh strength grew, more men were dropped in to Dien Bien Phu to bolster the French defenses.

RIGHT: Ten M24 Chaffee light tanks were the sole armored force available to de Castries.

high ground, while Giap's anti-aircraft guns were able to place a barrage of steel and high explosive above the dropping zones. The zones themselves were not always clearly marked, and the close proximity of the troops on the front lines made identification difficult for the harassed pilots. Small wonder that most of the supplies were dropped on to the Viet Minh lines, while many aircraft were shot down and the crews killed or captured.

With the airstrips closed, the wounded could no longer be evacuated and had to remain in the underground caves dug as a hospital. Four surgeons and one female nurse labored continuously, doing what they could with the dwindling stocks of drugs and medical supplies. There were only 40 beds, so new tunnels were dug into the clay, and the men just laid on shelves cut into the walls. The conditions soon

resembled a scene from some medieval view of hell, with filthy, bloodstained men lying in agony, some with maggots festering on their wounds. "We think they help prevent gangrene," said one doctor.

Early April heralded another Viet Minh offensive, with four days of bitter fighting around Elaine and Dominique. As the French perimeter shrunk, the difficulties of dropping supplies increased, forcing Bigeard to launch another counterattack into Elaine in an effort to clear a larger dropping zone. Every artillery piece still intact, together with all the infantry light mortars, fired into the one spot, to be followed by a desperate infantry attack from the French paras. A vicious hand-to-hand fight ensued, with men using clubs and daggers as well as their rifles, grenades and sub-machine guns. Eventually the French pushed the Vietnamese

ABOVE: During a lull in the fighting, wounded men are being cared for in the open. At first, the French wounded could be evacuated by air, but once the airstrip was closed they were trapped, along with their comrades.

out of their foxholes, although they had taken heavy casualties.

It was now the middle of April, and the French grimly held on to Isabelle and their central positions of Elaine, Huguette, Claudine and Francoise. There were a few men hanging on to the edge of Dominique, although this was now largely controlled by the Viet Minh. Giap's casualties had been immense, with his army now down to less than 40,000 effectives. Rather than press on blindly he took the decision to change to siege tactics while rebuilding his strength. So for the next few weeks, the Vietnamese dug a series of trenches around the French, extending them toward the center in a network of saps and dugouts. Short of ammunition, the defenders could not even harass the digging, instead they conserved their shells and bullets for the final assault which they knew must come soon.

Meanwhile the rest of the world watched the unfolding battle, with gloomy headlines about the inevitable fate of the defenders. The French made plans for a rescue mission, with a column of troops attempting to cross the jungle

from Laos, supported by commandos, but they had insufficient strength to fight their way past the Viet Minh Regiment sent to delay such an attempt. Western governments were also pressured by the French to help, who cited the onslaught of Communism in an attempt to get American support. President Eisenhower did consider applying US air power against Giap but political opposition persuaded him otherwise. Coincidentially, a conference of the major powers was scheduled in Geneva for 8 May, where issues such as the Vietnam conflict would be discussed. Ho Chi Minh and Giap were determined that the battle should be over by then, so that the world could be presented with a fait accompli.

Back in the French lines, the ragged, filthy exhausted men could only listen and watch as the enemy's trenches crept toward them. There was very little chance of any meaningful help being sent. Hanoi's contribution to their morale was to promote de Castries to General and cite every man for the Croix de Guerre. It was about all that Navarre could do for the beleaguered garrison.

FAR LEFT: Paras dive for cover as artillery shells come screaming in toward their positions.

BELOW: French air support was limited to bombs and strafing from F-8F Bearcats, operating from distant airfields. Over 30 were lost to anti-aircraft fire and bad weather.

ABOVE: *The battlefield soon took on the appearance of a blasted moonscape, with the defenders huddled in their trenches and bunkers.*

RIGHT: *After Dien Bien Phu fell, some of the wounded prisoners were repatriated by the Viet Minh.*

ABOVE: *Smoke shrouds the battlefield in the last few hours of resistance.*

LEFT: *French soldiers and their Vietnamese allies are led into captivity. Many would not return.*

157

The shelling started again on 5 May, when Giap's infantry came over the top in an overwhelming assault. The French positions were finally crumbling, with men just too physically exhausted to fight effectively. Bigeard and de Castries considered a suicidal plan for a breakout through Giap's lines, but soon realized that such an operation was beyond the capabilities of their men. The end was near, and on the 7th, de Castries transmitted the position to Hanoi. The reply was one that many soldiers would recognise – one that is typical of politicians who are refusing to come to terms with a situation that they have created. "You may stop fighting" de Castries was told, "But the white flag must not be flown above Dien Bien Phu." A few hours later, at 1750 hours, a young Viet Minh soldier with his sun helmet, black "pyjamas," sandals and Russian assault rifle entered de Castries' bunker and took all inside prisoner.

Around 5000 Frenchmen and their colonial allies had died, while over half of the remaining 10,000 were seriously wounded. Giap had lost some 8000, with another 15,000 wounded. The Viet Minh had won their victory though, one which spelt the end of French involvement in that troubled country and which led to the partition into north and south at Geneva. This would not be the end, however, and Giap would soon find himself up against a much more powerful western nation that had taken upon itself the role of the bastion against Communism. As for the 10,000 or so survivors of Dien Bien Phu, their suffering was by no means over. Led away on a nightmarish march into internment, many would die from exhaustion, malnourishment, illness and sheer neglect during their time in captivity. Three years later when they were released, less than a third of them came home.

BELOW: The Viet Minh delegation to ceasefire negotiations in Vietnam in July 1954. After Dien Bien Phu, these men held all the cards.

Index

Page numbers in *italics* refer to illustrations.

Acknowledgments

The author and publisher would like to thank Design 23, the designers; Stephen Small, the editor; Suzanne O'Farrell and Liz Montgomery, the picture researchers; Veronica Price and Nicki Giles for production; and Ron Watson for providing the index. The following individuals and agencies provided photographic material:

Africana Museum, pages: 104(bottom), 108
American Antiquarian Society, pages: 60
Ancient Art & Architecture, pages: 19(top)
Anne S. K. Brown Military Collection, pages: 62(bottom left & right), 64, 67, 74(both), 87, 94(right)
Archive Gerstenberg, pages: 130
Ashmolean Museum, Oxford, pages: 6
Associated Press, pages: 148, 151, 152(both), 154, 156(bottom)
Bettmann Archive, pages: 8, 9, 29, 35, 36(top right), 41, 53(bottom), 72 73(both), 75 (bottom),77 (both), 78(all three), 84, 88, 89(bottom), 93, 95, 97(top & bottom), 99, 101, 103, 113, 123(top), 126, 127(both), 129(both), 136(right), 137
Bettmann/Hulton, pages: 110,120, 125(bottom)
Bibliotheque Nationale, pages: 18(bottom), 19(bottom), 20(both), 23(top), 26(bottom), 31, 32, 34
Blair Castle, pages: 51(top left)
Bodelian Library, pages: 17 (bottom)
British Library, pages: 30
Brompton Books, pages: 1, 17(top), 23(bottom), 85, 90(bottom), 128(bottom), 146, 147(middle & bottom), 157(bottom)
Bundersarchive, pages: 131(bottom)
Canterbury Cathedral, pages: 26(top)
Codex/Chris Schuler, pages: 39
Daughters of the Republic of Texas Library, San Antonio, pages: 2-3, 79, 80, 81
Mike Dixon, pages: 11(top), 14(both), 15
Mary Evans Picture Library, pages: 59
Werner Forman Archive, pages: 10(bottom)
Sonia Halliday, pages: 10(top), 43
Hulton-Deutsch, pages: 21(top), 104(top), 107, 109, 111, 112, 114, 115, 116, 119(top), 122(bottom), 124, 125(top), 133(bottom), 147(right), 155, 158
Imperial War Museum, England, pages: 102, 118, 119(bottom), 121(both), 122(top), 12(bottom), 127(top), 128(top), 132(top), 134(top), 139(bottom)
A. F. Kersting, pages: 12(top), 16, 27, 36(bottom)
The Khalili Collection, pages: 37, 38, 42
Leeds City Art Gallery/Temple Newsam House, pages: 7
Library of Congress, pages: 82, 89(bttom)
Malta Tourist Board, pages: 40, 43, 44(both), 45(both), 46, 47
Mansell Collection, pages: 33, 36(top left), 53(top), 56, 57, 62(top)
National Army Museum, England, pages: 48, 52, 65(top), 70(both), 105, 106
National Maritime Museum, England, pages: 61, 66, 68, 69, 71
National Museum of Scotland, pages: 50(top), 51(top right)
Old Court House Museum collection, Vicksburg, Mississippi, pages: 86
Royale Armouries, Chartres, pages: 28
The Royal Collection, pages: 49, 54-5
Smithsonian Institution, pages: 94(top left & center left)
Springfield Armory, pages: 97(right)
UPI/Bettmann, pages: 4-5, 100, 132(bottom), 133(top), 134(bottom), 138(bottom), 142, 149(top), 150, 153, 156(top), 157(top)
U.S. Department of Defense, pages: 135, 136(top), 138(top), 139(top), 141(both), 143, 144, 145
U.S. National Archives, pages: 83, 90-1, 91(bottom), 92, 140
Dean & Chapter of Westminster Abbey, pages: 22
Jim Winkley, pages: 96(bottom)